PALM READING MADE EASY

BY

ELIZABETH P. HOFFMAN

AN ESSANDESS SPECIAL EDITION
NEW YORK

PALM READING MADE EASY

SBN: 671-10545-0

CONTENTS

INTRODUCTION

Have you ever really looked at your own hands? Without glancing at them now, do you know if they are the same size? Or the same shape? Are all of your nails formed the same way? What is their color: mottled or red? How do you carry your hands? Do you use them in casual conversation? Now take a good look, and see if your answers are correct.

Those hands are pictures of the real you, physically, mentally, and emotionally. People often wear masks on their faces, but rarely do they mask their hands. You doubtless judge people by their handshakes without even consciously thinking about it. A limp, lifeless touch makes you think of a "cold fish," while an overpowering grip will immediately make you raise your mental guard so that you are not overcome. A firm, even clasp welcomes you, but does not break down your natural reserves.

The characteristics, skills, and abilities expressed in your hands are like the stars in the study of astrology; they "impel"; they do not "compel." There is, as there should be, a great similarity between hand analysis and astrology: one confirms the other. Many terms and names have similar connotations. Gettings correlates the two studies in a beautifully illustrated book that graphically portrays this close relationship.[1]

References to palmistry, like those to astrology, are found in the literature and lore of many peoples. According to tradition, in the papyri of ancient Egypt we can find allusions to foretelling the future in this way. Early Chaldeans, Sumerians, and Babylonians are all

[1] Fred Gettings, **The Book of the Hand** (London: Paul Hamlyn, 1965).

1

credited with originating the art of palmistry. Aristotle's writings on the subject are the oldest whose authorship can be specifically identified. Gettings has devoted many pages of his volume to a carefully written history, for those who wish to investigate this phase of the subject.[2] In the Far East, astrology and palmistry are closely allied and treated with far more concern and respect than they are in the West. When an American girl was to wed the Prince of Sikkim, these sources were consulted to determine the most auspicious time for the nuptials.

Hands are mentioned in many ways in religious writings. Judaism provides the oft-quoted citation: "Length of days is in her right hand and in her left hand riches and honor."[3] Christianity utilizes the "laying on" of hands for blessing and spiritual healing. The shaking of hands when people meet or part, by offering the one that customarily would have borne weapons, symbolizes friendship. Hands signify prayer and reverence; who is not familiar with **Praying Hands** by Albrecht Durer? Physical death is depicted in films and drama by a hand falling inert.

Your own hands provide, to even a casual observer, more information about yourself than you generally care to share. And you can learn to more fully understand and interpret such information on your own hands and on the hands of others. With this skill, you will have the means of increasing your knowledge of yourself and of those around you. For a person's hands indeed tell who he really is.

---

[2] Gettings, **The Book of the Hand.**
[3] Prov. 3:16.

CHAPTER
ONE

BASIC HAND DEVELOPMENT

When you were born, your hands were like mirrors of each other, in size, in shape, in pattern, and in general development. With thumbs tucked carefully under curled fingers, they were like closed, little buds. As you inhaled your first breath, those fingers trembled and stretched. With your first hunger pangs, one thumb found its way to your mouth. In rest, your hands curled tightly again. During your first few months, those fingers and hands amused you when they came into your field of vision. Gradually, your nervous system learned how to control their random waving; your disciplining of your own body began in a real way. Those tiny hands already indicated what your basic nature was—warm, emotional, intellectual, energetic, passive, practical, or idealistic. By the time you reached your teens, your hands had developed all their basic forms and patterns.

As you mature in all other parts of your body, so do you grow in hand development. Between the ages of twelve and fifteen, the early teen years, your less dominant hand (for most people the left hand) achieves its final form and pattern. From that time on, for the rest of your life, it virtually will never change. If you gain fifty pounds, it will thicken; or if you lose fifty, it will thin out evenly. But the proportions and developments will remain constant, unless a change occurs that is so drastic as to change your destiny. Your dominant hand will change as you grow, develop, accept, or reject various courses of action.

All kinds of events and situations create differences between your two hands. Your less dominant one indicates your basic nature, without the veneer that civilization applies. Your dominant hand reflects your activities, thoughts, and personality traits. Family demands, geographical location, education, and finances are a few of the factors that may cause changes in your hands. For example, you may have been raised in a family that disapproved, for religious reasons, of dancing. Your less dominant hand will indicate your natural rhythm and harmony, your innate physical dexterity and ease of motion, and your emotional response to musical sounds—all skills essential to a dancer. These would be dormant in your dominant hand because they had not been developed, but they would still be present. Not long ago a man, whose clothing and calloused hands revealed his work to be in the laboring field, came for a hand reading. His transcendent aptitude for the field of the healing arts, particularly surgery, was most evident, yet he had not pursued this profession. Questioning revealed that he was a butcher. He had completed high school in the early 1930s and there was no money available to him for further education. His desire to be a doctor completely thwarted, he entered the meat-packing business and used his skills there. He managed the first-aid station at his plant. The emergency room at the nearby hospital soon learned that the injuries he had treated needed little or no additional attention. Finances and education had kept him from his natural field, but his innate skill came through nevertheless.

Or consider this: If you were in Philadelphia and wanted to go to Pittsburgh and you consulted a map, you would probably choose to travel via the turnpike, but you wouldn't have to. You might prefer to travel across Route 30 through Gettysburg, Chambersburg, and over the mountains. Or you might elect to drive across Route 22 through Harrisburg. You could decide to travel south to Washington, D.C., if you chose, then drive to West Virginia and backtrack to Pittsburgh. The decision would be yours.

Your hands are maps in just the same way. Your less dominant hand is the map of your journey through life, showing routes you will probably take, while your dominant hand indicates the road you are actually following.

Physically, the human hand is one of the most fascinating parts of the body. Its usefulness is directed from the mind. Its very movements are controlled by the brain of the person it serves. The sensitive fingertips tell us about the world that they feel. Sympathy, love, and friendship are expressed through the touch of a hand. "Handmade" suggests not only the quality of a piece of needlework or woodwork, but denotes the love and personal concern accompanying it.

Hands are more sensitive to their physical surroundings, because of their makeup, than other parts of our bodies. On a wintry day, our fingers are cold even when encased in fur-lined gloves, while our cheeks remain rosy and warm although exposed to the elements. The elasticity of the skin, as we expand and contract our hands a hundred or more times a day, is amazing in itself. Callouses on the hands reveal their own stories. Nervous disorders and other illnesses make imprints on hands. We are able to note how ready a child is for school by the way he uses his hands. When he grasps a pencil or crayon in a fist and exerts great concentration and energy to guide it, we learn something of his muscle and nerve maturity. Then, as that hand uses the same instrument by learning to balance it between the thumb and index finger, we know that his controls are maturing. The use of scissors and other tools can indicate the same kinds of maturity. Skills in our hands reflect growth of the mind.

You doubtless know many people whose conversations would be severely handicapped if they could not use their hands. Smokers who have tried to "break the habit" frequently note that they don't know what to do with their hands without a cigarette or pipe to hold.

As you begin to study hands, it might be helpful to make a checklist, or chart, to assist you in remembering what to observe and correlate. (See Hand Analysis

Checklist in the Appendix.) With a little practice, you will begin to remember and be able to put together mounts, lines, shapes, and their meanings. In addition to this, on a sheet of plain paper, make an outline of your own hands by sketching around them. Then label the various parts as we identify them. You might like to have several outlines so that you can use one for mounts, one for lines, and one for general terms.

Your own hands will be the easiest to use for identification but the hardest for interpretation, because you will see in yourself only what you really want to see. You will be blind to other facets of yourself. This is true of all of us. Someone paraphrased Burns's famous poem to read, "Would God the gift to others gie, To see myself as I see me."

On your chart, first identify the palm itself, the solid area from the wrist to the base of the fingers. The side below the little finger is called the percussion side because it is the striking side; the thumb side is called the inner side. The palm area is where the lines are found that are generally thought to be the most revealing features. But although these lines do tell their own story, they are not in themselves worthy of prime consideration. However, we will use them as landmarks. Not every hand will reveal all of these lines clearly marked. On some they will be merged, on others they may be partially or entirely missing. What this signifies will be discussed later.

The first line begins between the thumb and the index finger, circles around the thumb, and then curves toward the wrist. This is the life line. The head line begins with the life line or just above it. It cuts into the middle of the palm, then may curve downward toward the life line or flow toward the percussion side of the hand. The third major line, the heart line, commences under the index or middle finger, then cuts across the upper part of the hand toward the little finger. This line frequently reaches completely across the hand and bends around the edge. The destiny, fate, career, or ambition line, call it what you will, starts near the wrist, rises vertically into the palm, then generally bends toward either the index or middle finger. It may have several branches, merge with other lines such as the life line, or start and stop at various intervals. Its variations are myriad. These four are the major lines. Many secondary or lesser lines, such as the Girdle of Venus, and marriage or affection lines will be identified as they are discussed.

Below the palm, across the wrist, are lines called rascettes, or bracelets. If you bend your hand forward, they will become prominent.

Now let us identify the fingers. These take their names from mythology, again a practice followed in common with astrology. Jupiter, the king of the gods, has provided the name for the index finger. Saturn is the middle digit, while Apollo, the ruler of the sun, is the name of the ring finger. The little finger reflects the properties of Mercury, the messenger god. The thumb does not have a special name, but stands on its own. At the base of each finger is a small fleshy area called a mount. These mounts take the name of the finger under which they are found: Jupiter, Saturn, Apollo, or Mercury. Some mounts may be high, others pushed together, while on a few hands they may be nonexistent.

In addition to these mounts below the fingers, there are five others to identify. At the base of the thumb is an area generally marked off from the rest of the palm by the life line. This area is called the Mount of Venus, named for the goddess of love and beauty. Above this mount and below the Jupiter mount is the Lower Mount of Mars. On the opposite, or percussion, side of the hand, just below the Mount of Mercury, is the Upper Mount of Mars. Beneath this one, on the lower part of the percussion side, is the Mount of the Moon, or Lunar mount. Across the base of the palm, separating it from the wrist, lies a small mount, if it exists at all, called the Neptune mount.

To return to the fingers, if you examine them, you will recognize that they are made up of three parts; these are called phalanges. The Mount of Venus is really the first phalange of the thumb. Phalanges are numbered from one to three beginning with the one nearest the palm. Nails are on the third phalange.

Several facts should be noted as you begin your study. First, don't jump to conclusions too quickly. You wouldn't trust a doctor who diagnosed your illness as pneumonia if all you told him over the phone was that you had a temperature of 102°. If he saw you in person, he could note your breathing, flushed countenance, and other signs that would suggest to his practiced eye that pneumonia could be your problem; but even so, he would follow this with additional checks and tests. In the same way, a good student of hands will note a characteristic in one part of the hand, then search for confirming signs or marks in another. The apparent absence of a heart line, for example, does not mean the subject has no emotions.

Second, be sure to examine both hands. Accidents and deformities leave records on hands and must be considered in an overall interpretation. Records that are destroyed through an accident to the hand will rewrite themselves on an uninjured part.

Third, develop the habit of observing hands wherever you go. Watch the man who services your car, the checker who rings up your groceries, and the waitress who serves you at lunch. Notice how they carry their hands, and their size and general shape. With a little practice, you will be able to learn a lot about people so that you can work and live with them with sympathy and understanding.

CHAPTER
TWO

HAND TYPES AND WHAT
THEY TELL US

Now that you can find your way around a hand "geographically," we are going to begin to study it as a unit, as well as through its various components. Both kinds of information are necessary for a complete evaluation. Actually, you really begin to "read a palm" from the first moment you see a person.

Benham, in his book **The Laws of Scientific Hand Reading**, devotes an entire chapter to the "pose and carriage of the hands" that merits careful study by anyone whose work brings him into close contact with other people.[1] He describes fifteen basic hand positions and outlines the characteristics they represent. However, for our purpose, general observation will suffice. Do the hands you are about to examine play a

---

[1] William Benham, **The Laws of Scientific Hand Reading** (New York: Duell, Sloan and Pearce, 1946).

part in their owner's conversation, or do they relax quietly until you are ready to examine them? When you are approached by a person whose hands are at his sides and whose arms move in a relaxed, easy manner, you can be sure these hands are reflecting his own inner relaxation. But if they are hanging limp and flaccid, they reveal that their owner is indecisive and flaccid, too.

Individuals whose hands are clenched reveal tensions. If the thumbs are tucked inside the fingers (the way a small baby makes a fist), we know that the owner is insecure and is looking for something to grasp for assurance and confidence. Whether this is a temporary attitude or a definite part of his personality can be determined by other signs. When the thumbs are outside the clenched fingers, belligerence or animosity is expressed. Some people have hands that dart and wave about as they talk or listen. These hands are antennae, reaching out to absorb and pull in information from their surroundings. Some people try to hide their hands, putting them behind their backs or thrusting them into pockets. They, too, are feeling unsure and uncertain. They want to be coaxed or wheedled into offering their hands, even though they may be very desirous of having you look at them. By forcing you to reach out for their hands, they have increased their own feeling of confidence and importance——they have something someone else wants. This is observable even in casual hand shaking when you meet a person. Almost everyone knows someone who resembles Dickens' famous Uriah Heep, a man epitomized by his obsequious display of hands, revealing the sly, untrustworthy, cruel depths of his character.

My almost instant dislike of a new employee in my company was engendered by this kind of hand display as we carried on our first conversation. At the earliest opportunity, I studied his hands (without his knowledge, of course). This confirmed my original impression of a man not to be trusted, one who would use any person or means to achieve his own ends. Time has confirmed this. He used the work of other people to promote himself, until he attempted it with someone who realized what was happening and trapped him. Thus, careful observation of the carriage and use of hands can give you solid information.

As you reach out and touch the hands you are examining, look at both the palm, or front, and the back. Observe any scars or deformities; these should be noted in your reading. Characteristics that would have been revealed on a missing or misshapen area will show themselves elsewhere. If scar tissue in any appreciable amount conceals a marking, that characteristic will be emphasized in another part of the hand. A Mercury mount with a heavy scar may have a blurred medical stigmata (three vertical lines) (see illustration page 105), but this healing ability will reveal itself through the fingertips, the emotional and mental lines, and the intuition lines.

Now you want to note the size, texture, and flexibility of the hands. Size is the clue to many characteristics. A hand should be in general proportion to body build. An average hand should measure the same from wrist bracelet to longest fingertip as the subject's face. Very large or very small hands are easy to identify; those more nearly average require more careful scrutiny.

Ask your subject to close his fingers over his palm to see how close to the wrist they reach. Short hands will not be able to get near to the wrist, while large ones may reach even past it. Check both hands. In a medium-sized hand, the width of the palm is slightly less than the length of it. If the fingers are in proportion, the Saturn finger's length will equal the width across the top of the hand. Short fingers are usually found on broad palms—those as wide as, or wider than, they are long. Small hands tell us their owner can work with big ideas or large projects. Small-handed people generally have a childlike exuberance to bring to their tasks. A vivid imagination generally accompanies small hands. This helps their owners to dream and to plan. Large hands are found on people who can work competently with details. They can organize the components of the small-handed director's program. When a woman with small hands desires a special dress for a grand occasion, she will select a fine pattern or design and suitable fabric. If she makes the garment herself (and her hands will reveal whether or not she should attempt it), she'll complain about attaching the zipper or fitting the gussets. The hem won't be finished until the day she actually needs the dress. These details don't interest her, only the total impression. But the woman with large hands will delight in the fine turning at the neckline and the carefully stitched buttonholes.

Think of the various organizations and clubs to

which you belong. They will operate most successfully when the president has small hands that attest to his ability to develop well-rounded programs. The secretary and treasurer, by contrast, should have large hands that bespeak skill in maintaining accurate, detailed records. Or consider for a moment the men who repair your car. The mechanic who can quickly diagnose the cause of its faulty performance will have small hands, but the man who installs the rebuilt transmission should have veritable hams at the ends of his arms.

Have you ever noticed that the most gentle and meticulous dentists have huge hands?

The breadth of the hand as well as the length gives insight into personality. If a hand is broad as well as small, the owner will be energetic and impulsive. These characteristics will also show up in line markings, but can be checked as basic traits here. People with small, broad hands can, when they have to, complete their work. Those with narrow hands find this most difficult.

An average-sized hand, neither large nor small, shows that the owner can handle a job in his field and complete it without outside supervision. He will notice that his hedge along the sidewalk needs cutting; he'll trim it, clean up the clippings, and oil his shears so they'll be ready for use the next time, all as a matter of course, without prodding from his wife or mother.

As mentioned before, many persons have hands that do not match in size. This indicates a major change in their development since childhood. When the less dominant hand, usually the left, is noticeably smaller than the other, it indicates that the owner has been forced to pay attention to what he considers mundane details in his daily activities. The owner of a large less dominant hand and a small dominant one has had to acquire the ability to absorb large blocks of information or the skills to perform a task superficially without perfecting every component or detail.

The color and texture of the skin on the hands will give you the next clues to their owner's personality. The back of the hand is the best place to check on texture. If the skin is sensitive and fine, it reveals a person aware of softness and delicacy in everything about him. Even if he were a cruel person (and this would show up in other areas), he would be cruel in a subtle, indirect way. A woman murderer whose hands were fine-skinned, for example, dispatched her victims by shooting strychnine into chocolates and then returning the candy to the store, reporting that the wrong ones had been delivered to her. To what depths can subtlety go!

Conversely, heavy-grained, thick skin indicates stiffness in its owner. The lack of refinement will be reflected in the various facets of the individual's personality. A man with coarse, heavy skin would never be interested in listening to a Mozart concerto. The texture of the skin must be remembered as you diagnose other hand characteristics, because it will emphasize or modify them. For example, fine-textured skin on a dominant Jupiter hand will make its owner less domineering; rough texture will make the Jupiter hand more tyrannical. Delicate skin will help the creative musician to work with compositions for a string quartet, while heavy skin will indicate his skill in creating military marches.

Be sure to allow for your subject's age when checking skin for dryness. Older people have drier skin than young ones. Moist palms indicate tension. Your client may be concerned about what you will or will not reveal. Damp hands also are found on people who work and produce well under pressure. As long as they don't have a deadline to meet, they tend to loaf along, keeping moderately busy. But when a report comes due or their boss comes up with a job to be done "yesterday," they can meet the challenge. If their hands are large and moist, the tasks will be conscientiously done; if the hands are small and damp, it will be done reluctantly, solely because of outside pressure from a superior.

Skin color provides more clues to personality. Red hands, red lines, and bright nails go with an individual full of vigor and intensity. Everything that their owner does he does at full speed: he eats heartily, he loves vigorously, he plays with great energy. However, this does not mean everything is executed with skill—other parts of the hand will reveal whether or not this is so.

Pink hands generally belong to healthy people. They enjoy living and pass that feeling of enjoyment to those around them. Their warmth and optimism radiate and sparkle. Regardless of race, pink palms and hands are a fortunate possession.

In contrast are white hands. Frequently, artists depict long, narrow, white hands to symbolize saints or similar people who spend their lives in contemplation, implying that this type of hand has a saintly virtue. Actually, a white hand—and, as before, this refers primarily to the palm—belongs to someone with a cold, impersonal, unemotional outlook. Although he may be dreamy and visionary, he would tend to be cold. If the religious or philosophic side of his nature is strong, he would be a mystic. A white Saturn-dominated hand always denotes a melancholy out-look——one who sees a glass as half empty rather than half full. This hand will never have a strong Mount of Venus; love and affection to that extent are impossible.

Sometimes, and we hope very rarely, you will come upon blue hands. These indicate circulatory troubles. It would be most unwise to tell your subject that he undoubtedly has a serious health problem, but it would be prudent to suggest to someone close to him that you had identified a situation that needed attention. Blue nails also indicate a lack of oxygen in the blood. A few years ago, I observed the hands of a friend on a Saturday evening. She confessed to feeling very tired. Her nails were quite blue and her hands were ex-tremely cold, even though she had been playing an organ. I suggested to her husband that she should see a doctor quickly. He reported that they were to have dinner the next day with their family physician, who was also a personal friend. But a phone call late the next evening informed me that my friend had died of a heart attack in a taxi en route home from the doctor.

As you check the color of the palm, test it also for flexibility. Stiff, rigid hands reflect those same ten-dencies in their owner. If the fingers curl in toward the palm, forming a kind of cup, you can be sure that their owner is cautious, is slow to try new ventures or new ideas, and is generally unprogressive, no matter what his field. Some hands will open and extend full-size easily. Their owners are quietly secure in their own **modus operandi.** They are sympathetic to those around them, but have little desire to create any changes. Not spendthrifts, they can and will hold on to their possessions, both emotional and mental as well as physical, unless their fingers are spread apart. In that case, if the spacing is even, we have spendthrifts—those who will lavish time and energy as well as, on occasion, money.

Some hands will be extremely flexible. You can bend back the fingers until they form a high arch, without hurting their owner. This same flexibility will be found in the owner's mental and emotional makeup. He will fit into any situation in which he finds himself. He will listen to both sides of an argument carefully before making up his own mind. He likes to do many things and to do them as simultaneously as possible.

As in other traits, be sure to check flexibility of both hands—they may not be the same. The dominant hand shows the subject as he is now, the less dominant as he is by nature. He may have changed—and that in itself is important.

Now you should be ready to identify the hands you are studying by shape. A good hand analyst will compare right and left hands to determine what differences exist, for the experience of living can cause the dominant hand to change, as we have noted. Basically, hands fall into six categories:

1. Elementary
2. Square
3. Spatulate
4. Conic
5. Pointed
6. Mixed

On pages 21–26, you will find drawings of these six basic types.

Fred Gettings relates hand classifications to the four basic elements that we generally associate with astrology: earth, fire, air, and water.[2] He explains how hands reflect the characteristics symbolized in the ancient divisions propounded by the physician Galen. However, almost all other students of the art use the six groupings listed above.

As you initiate your classification of hands that you observe, note that very seldom will you find a perfect example of any of the types, but that, nonetheless, most will be readily identifiable.

Elementary hands (see illustration page 21) are found almost entirely among men. You will seldom find their owners asking to have their palms read—they never heard of such a thing, or if they have, they don't believe it possible and it is, therefore, not worth their time. These palms are thick, hard, and quite large. The fingers are small, broad, firm to the point of stiffness; the thumb short, thick, and probably turning back a bit. All of the fingers on an elementary hand will be short, shorter than the palm and very similar to each other in length. If the joints are predominantly smooth, the owner of this hand will be easier to work with than if they are knotted. The skin will be hard, perhaps even horny; the back of the hand will have heavy pore markings. All of the nails will be short, broad, and thick. On the palms, line markings will tend to extremes—very few or so many that they appear to be inked on. A sparsity of lines is the

<hr>

[2] Gettings, **The Book of the Hand.**

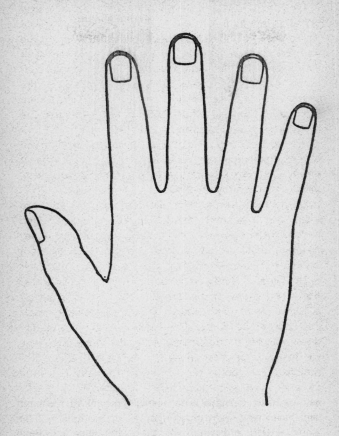

ELEMENTARY HAND AND FINGERS

21

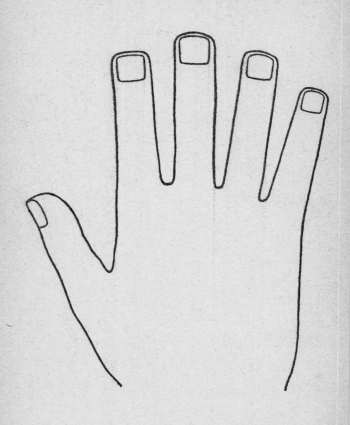

SQUARE HAND AND FINGERS

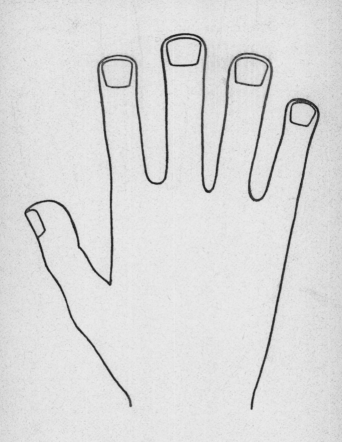

SPATULATE HAND AND FINGERS

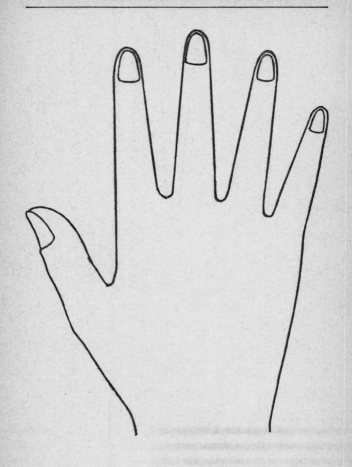

CONIC HAND AND FINGERS

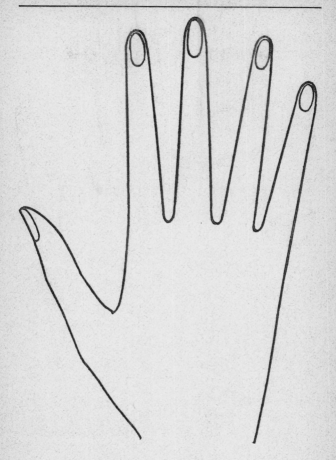

POINTED HAND AND FINGERS

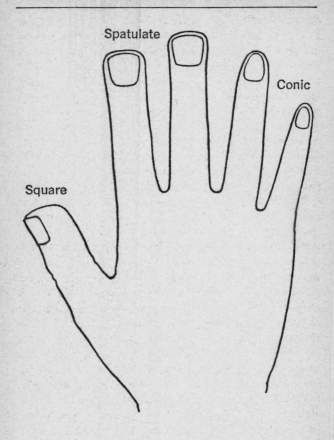

Spatulate

Conic

Square

MIXED HAND AND FINGERS

general rule. Owners of these hands have no imagination or ambition. They have accepted the ready-made ideas, opinions, and directions that were presented to them in their youth from persons in authority—generally their parents or teachers. They excel at unskilled labor. Routine is necessary to them. Elementary hands will mow your lawn or shovel your sidewalk, but don't let them prune your roses—no bushes will be left when they are finished. They make good stock boys, lugging cartons or shelving merchandise. Repair or maintenance crews need some of these people. But Heaven help your car when they work in parking lots!

Square hands (see illustration page 22) are those whose palms are as broad as they are long. On these, the fingers are short—the solid part of the hand is longer than the digits and frequently contains a deep hollow. Most of the fingers will be square-shaped at the tip. The skin will be firm and somewhat elastic. Lines are somewhat more numerous here than on the elementary hand. Again, the thumb will be short. The physical energy in the hand transmits itself to those who touch it. When we shake a male hand of this type, we mentally react: "truck driver!" Square hands may be symbolized by earth—they are practical, useful, life-giving, conservative. Their owner likes beauty and harmony around him, in his home and in his work. Moderation is a key word to his interests and activities. He performs best when he understands what is expected of him. He has a dedicated sense of duty and generally respects authority. The fingers on a square hand may modify or vary some of these general characteristics. Square-hand owners like to "possess" things; the men are good providers and the women competent homemakers and shoppers. Both are workers in whatever fields they find themselves. Seldom do they show much ambition or drive.

Turning our attention to spatulate hands (see illustration page 23), we find we identify them as those that are wider at the base of the fingers than at the wrist. The fingers are similar in length to the palm, or a bit longer. The nails will be thinner in texture than those on a square or elemental palm. Knotted joints create a problem for these people. The thumbs are well formed and often quite thick through the middle phalange. The nails are generally spatulate also—wider at the top than at the matrix. The owners of these hands forge ahead with great drive. They generally combine endurance along with good mental and physical skills. They are usually enterprising and can find new ways to tackle old problems; their extraordinary energy wears out their associates. When combined with artistic skills, these people will be in the avant-garde. People with spatulate hands need to have their work and accomplishments recognized. Thank your spatulate-handed public-relations man for preparing a good story, and he will be eager to do another, even better. As a company manager, he'll be able to keep an eye on the many phases of the business at the same time. Select a gal for the committeewoman in your political precinct—she'll see that your needs come to the attention of the proper individual. Or shop in a supermarket that has a manager of this type—the store will be clean, well stocked, and will always offer the newest types and brands of merchandise. Many women would like husbands from this group—they're good "do-it-yourselfers."

Regarding the philosophic hand, as it's referred to in some books on palmistry, we look for hands with large thumbs, knotted joints, and generally angular appearance. In reality, this is usually a modification of either the spatulate or conic hand. However, it emphasizes mental and emotional skills rather than physical ones. Although it is generally large, it is pliable. By looking at conic, or artistic hands, as they are sometimes called, we can learn to identify philosophic hands as those that fall between them and spatulate ones.

Conic hands, as the name implies (see illustration page 24) taper slightly from the wrist to the base of the fingers. These digits also show the same narrowing effect throughout their length. The outer edge of this hand is somewhat curved. The whole hand will be flexible and soft, but not flabby to the touch. A variety of thumbs are found here. These people are mental rather than physical in their outlook and activities. Usually, they speak or write competently. They like to work, play, and generally live freely, without time clocks or routine schedules. They are planners, instructors. These people are influenced by music, color, and even growing plants in their surroundings. Play recorded music where they work, and they will produce better results. A potted plant on a conic-handed executive's or secretary's desk will improve his performance and his attitude. See that your conic-handed child has a bright room, and his disposition will be sunnier.

29

The pointed hand (see illustration page 25) is really an extension of the conic one. It can be identified by its long palm and long, slim fingers. The skin will be soft and delicate and probably very white. Women's hands of this type are very narrow. Owners of this hand are generally difficult to live and work with because of their idealistic approach to all facets of life. The poet who was content to sit beneath the bough with a "loaf of bread" and a "jug of wine" undoubtedly had pointed hands. A "hyacinth for his soul" would be adequate food. These impractical people provide dreams for the rest of us.

Mixed hands (see illustration page 26) obviously are combinations of some or all of these varieties. The fingers will represent several types and will contrast with the shape of the palm. These people are usually pliable or adaptable to any situation; but, depending on what the details of the hands reveal, they frequently waste their efforts because they are "jacks of all trades and masters of none."

Perhaps this example will illustrate how these various types can work together: Imagine that you own a company that produces candy. You will hire workmen with elementary palms for routine maintenance duties. Some of them will work on the loading docks, and others will carry out routine chores. The next group, those with square hands, will care for the mixing machines, the molding equipment; they will work in the wrapping and packing areas. The clerks and stenos in the business offices will have square hands. Physical duties requiring little mental activity best suit their interests and skills. They will not chafe over the monotony of the daily duties and will carry out directions unquestioningly. Supervising these employees and generally managing the entire plant will be those with spatulate hands. These workers will oversee practical activities; they generally combine manual and mental skills and can readily locate and identify problems. The secretaries in the business office, the leading sales manager, and the office supervisors will also have spatulate hands.

The general manager and division director should have conic hands, fingers, and nails. These professionals design new product lines, recommend advertising programs, plan personnel training and supervisory procedures. Their work will be primarily mental and will not be governed by a clock. Then, finally, one or, at the most, two people should be employed who have pointed hands. They will dream up new products, new sources of materials, novel ways of packaging, or unusual methods of improving the company. Most of their ideas will not be practical, but the employees with spatulate, conic, or mixed hands will winnow through their suggestions to determine which have real merit.

CHAPTER
THREE

THE THUMB AND ITS IMPORTANCE

Centuries ago, gladiators looked to the patron of the games in the arenas for a sign to tell whether or not they should slay their vanquished opponent. "They win applause by slaying with a turn of the thumb."[1] Thumbs up meant life, and thumbs down, death. Some palmists feel that they can give an accurate reading of a person's characteristics from their thumbs alone. While that isn't recommended, nonetheless, thumbs do merit careful study as the most important digit on your hand. Tuck the thumb on your dominant hand against the palm, and hold it there. Now try to pick up a pencil or turn a page in this book. Even simple tasks like these become difficult and awkward and sometimes even impossible without the use of a thumb.

---

[1] Juvenal, **Satires**, Book III.

Recall the last time you injured your thumb; it may have been a small cut or a simple bruise that you suffered, but nonetheless it made you aware of how often you used your thumb and how troublesome a sore one becomes. Think of the last tiny baby you saw. His little fists carefully concealed his thumbs. When he became hungry and no food was immediately offered, he tried to find solace by sucking his thumb. As he matured, that thumb gradually left its hiding place under the fingers and curled beside them. Watch a toddler "write." He seizes his crayon or pencil with his fist and then attempts to balance the tool with his thumb. As his muscles and nerves mature and his mental powers become more adept at giving directions, his hand will assume a more nearly normal writing position. The control of the hand motion reflects mental growth and nerve discipline.

Examine carefully both of the thumbs you are studying. Note any difference in their length or shape. Are they the same thickness? Do they extend from your hand at the same angle? We'll discuss what these characteristics mean as we go along. Keep in mind that the thumb on your less dominant hand reveals your basic characteristics, or traits, while that on your dominant hand announces any changes. These thumbs deliver quite a message about their owner to a student of palms.

At first glance, it would seem that the thumb has two phalanges, in contrast to the three on the other fingers. Actually, the thumb has a special set of muscles and a joint situated between one of the carpal bones of the wrist and one of the metacarpal bones in the palm. This enables the thumb to touch the front of every other finger, the only digit that can do this. As you examine your own hand, you can feel how the bones of your thumb meet the bone that lies under the Mount of Venus. The size of the thumb should first be noted. Length and thickness as well as position on the hand must be considered. An average to long thumb will come at least halfway up the lowest phalange of the index, or Jupiter, finger. Some thumbs are so short that they scarcely reach the bottom of this digit. Check to see the set of the thumb on the hand. A high-set thumb may seem to be long, but it really isn't. In addition, check the width or thickness. A very thin thumb, even though it may be long, does not qualify as a large one. The thickness or width should be in proportion to the length.

Tradition insists, and study bears it out, that possessors of large, well-balanced thumbs are strong in character——whether or not this strength is used for good depends on what you find in the rest of the hand. These people can use their heads. Small-thumbed people are led by their emotions, and they like to be supervised by large-thumbed people. The possessors of small thumbs are more romantically inclined than large-thumbed ones. Really great, productive people have large, balanced thumbs. Even though serious problems may be revealed in other parts of the hand, the large thumb indicates sufficient strength and drive to consciously overcome them. Observe how close the thumb lies to the palm as the hand is relaxed. The more introverted or self-centered a person is, the closer the thumb to the palm. A closely curled hand (in a relaxed state) reveals an insecure person. What kind of fist do you make when danger threatens? Thumbs in or out? If it's in, you doubtless retreat either mentally or physically until someone helps to cope with the problem. If it's out, make sure your belligerence is justified and that you can defend your position.

On some people's hands the thumb lies close to the palm even in a relaxed situation. These individuals are conventional in attitudes, opinions, and appearance. Conversely, a wide-set thumb emphasizes independence in these same areas. Extremely liberal thinkers have "wide open" thumbs. Some young people have recently adopted the popular long-haired, carelessly dressed appearance, thinking that by this means they are expressing their dislike for more traditional customs. But a glance at the hands of a goodly number of these people reveals closed, curled thumbs, indicating that they are really searching for acceptance. In addition, a low-set thumb indicates that its owner has a real sympathy for all kinds of needs; the other parts of the hand will suggest the area that appeals to him most: economic, medical, emotional, and so on. These people are ready to espouse causes that aid others.

Some thumbs are supple, others rigid. If the low-set thumb is flexible, generous activities will be conducted with warmth and personal interest. A rigid, low-set thumb will indicate that while the owner may participate in a philanthropic activity in a very energetic way, he will do it for selfish reasons. His boss may be impressed with the organizational ability he demonstrates and give him more responsibility with a corresponding pay raise. The long-thumbed person would head the campaign drive just because it would benefit many people and his special talents could help. Most liberal thinkers in politics, religion, and education have low-set thumbs, but the length of the thumbs are clues to their motives. Some palmists feel that low-set thumbs denote superior mental ability, but this is not always the case.

Now check to see if the thumb has a "waist" (see illustration page 39). Does it narrow in the second phalange so that it resembles an hour-glass figure? Thumbs that are thick through the second phalange indicate that the owners are strong on determination and quick in judgment. Those who don't agree with these people with "waisted" thumbs are inclined to call them stubborn. The latter seem to be dogmatic, and, frequently, they absolutely refuse to change their minds. Such a person will say, "I'm determined," but an observer will say, "he's stubborn." A person with a waisted thumb should be plied with reasons—logical, orderly reasons for the activity or attitude desired of him. If he understands and accepts the logic, he will do whatever is desired; but if he doesn't, he won't. The owners of the "determined" thumbs will react more intuitively when making decisions or working out situations than waisted-thumb owners. If the first, or nail, phalange is noticeably longer than the second, it emphasizes the stubbornness.

Two words, "will" and "logic," are always used in connection with the thumb in books and articles on palm reading. The nail phalange is frequently called the "will" phalange. As previously stated, it emphasizes the determination represented by a thick thumb. The shape of this first phalange also provides information for you. The nail and the fingertip may follow one of the general hand shapes: square, spatulate, conic, or pointed, or the nail phalange occasionally is clubbed, which is instantly identified because of the way it splays out about the second phalange. It may be broad and flat or very convex. It shows violence and cruelty, but not necessarily in a physical way. However, all possessors of clubbed thumbs have violent tempers, even though they may deny it or have learned to discipline their outbursts. One possessor of such a thumb delighted in encouraging people in all sorts of ventures, promising assistance, until it was needed. Then he would turn his back on the situation he had helped to create and would delight in watching a former protegé lose his possessions in a financial debacle or fail in a business venture when promised support never materialized. Another owner of such a thumb, in the real estate business, thoroughly enjoyed encouraging clients to try to finance a home they couldn't possibly afford. It goes without saying that no one needs a doctor or dentist with this kind of thumb.

Square-shaped "will" phalanges show that their owners possess common sense and practicality. Spatulate tips indicate a person of action. Depending on the rest of the thumb, this may be impulsive and active and, therefore, indicates a person who leaps before he looks. If this phalange is very long, the spatulate tip indicates that the owner can prevent his own success by moving too quickly, either mentally or physically, depending on his bent. A conic tip cautions its owner and makes him more aware of other people's needs and desires. Pointed tips are found on impressionable people and detract from their determination.

The second phalange—the "logic" one—in addition to what it reveals by the presence or absence of a waist, indicates how much common sense its owner possesses or uses. Short-phalanged people generally lack common sense and physical energy. A long area implies tactfulness and diplomacy.

On some hands, you will find very flexible thumbs: they can be bent backward easily without pain or discomfort. Impulsiveness will dominate in this person, in either physical, mental, or emotional activity, depending upon his bent. Often this person is a spendthrift, and this, too, will show in the other fingers. Although the subject may be versatile, he will need discipline to bring his goals to fruition. Conversely if the thumb is very stiff or rigid you can be sure you are dealing with a stingy person. The term "stiff-necked" could be changed to "stiff-thumbed" and carry the same connotation. But on the positive side, stiff-thumbed people have a strong sense of justice.

Now look at the palm with the fingers up, and examine the edge of the thumb as it comes from the wrist area. Angles that are formed by the metacarpal bone are known as the angles of rhythm (the lower one near the wrist) and harmony (the upper one near the base of the second phalange). (See illustration page 39.) These two terms are generally associated with music; but here their meanings, while allied to the arts, go further. Rhythm in music is a patterned or repetitive beat or accent. It tells us whether a composition is a march, a waltz, or a dirge. A well-formed angle of rhythm is found on a person who needs his life to move in rhythm or in a pattern. He responds to various parts of the day; he needs to live in an area where climate changes with the seasons. Southern Florida is not a satisfying place for him. If the rest of his hand indicates artistic talent, this will strengthen it. A possessor of a strong angle of rhythm will usually relax easily to music, and even sleep better with a radio playing quietly. Harmony may be defined as a pleasing combination of tones, colors, shapes, and so on. The possessors of a well-defined angle of harmony will develop headaches or upset stomachs or other physical discomforts if they spend much time in a

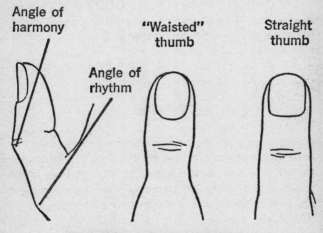

Angle of harmony

Angle of rhythm

"Waisted" thumb

Straight thumb

VARIOUS THUMB ELEMENTS

room painted in a color that clashes with the furnishings. Harmony angles denote a need to work and live in a community or mental climate where the owner is with people and surroundings like himself or that complement him. A scientist with mathematical skills can work well in a large university department with people of similar inclinations, but would be very lonely on a faculty of a small liberal arts school where he was the only instructor in his field. When both angles are strong in a hand, you are working with a person who responds to order and balance in all areas of life and not just the arts.

In summarizing your examination, keep in mind the following points: size, shape of both phalanges, and flexibility. Are the basic angles prominent? There is a reproduction that comes to mind of a colonial tavern sign picturing a hand with a bandaged thumb. If you had to examine a palm with such a thumb you would work under a severe handicap—thumbs tell so much about their owners.

CHAPTER
FOUR

THE FINGERS

Do you recall the painting of the **Creation** by Michelangelo in the Sistine Chapel? Adam, in a semirecumbent position, is reaching out with his left hand, index finger partially extended, toward the Deity. As the Creator bends toward Adam with His right hand stretched forth, His index finger is nearly touching that of the first man. Some people aver that this painting depicts an old belief that the spark of life passes into the body of a baby at birth through his fingers. We do know that as a newborn infant cries, his fingers usually jerk open and move. During the first hours of life, those same fingers can grasp an object and bear the baby's weight.

In your own mind, think of fingers as streams or cables of energy. Currents of emotional sensitivity and awareness enter you through your fingertips and flow into the palm, down across the wrist, and into the rest of your body. The shape, form, and position of the fingers indicate how easily these streams can flow. Smooth fingers allow them to pass through with virtually undiminished strength. Knots on either the upper or lower joints or both are barriers that slow up the movement. Longitudinal markings, if there are only one or two, on the fingers or the mounts at their bases strengthen the characteristics represented. Several parallel lines dissipate the force. Horizontal lines weaken these same traits—they are barriers, or obstacles, to be overcome.

As you begin to examine the fingers on a hand, observe how they are spaced. Ask your subject to hold up his hand in front of you with the palm facing you. Or hold your own in this way. Notice the space between the fingers. Are they close together? Or evenly spaced? Are some gaps wider than others? (See illustration page 43.) Each formation has its own meaning. A wide space between the thumb and index finger indicates that the hand belongs to a person who values his independence and freedom, no matter what his field. If the thumb is held close to the palm, it indicates that its owner holds strong opinions on any subject that arouses his interest. A wide space between Jupiter (the index finger) and Saturn (the middle finger) symbolizes independence or freedom of thought. The owner of a hand with this structure likes to think things through for himself. Many times his thoughts are liberal or broad, even beyond generally recognized norms. If there is also a wide space between Apollo and Mercury on this hand, then the per-

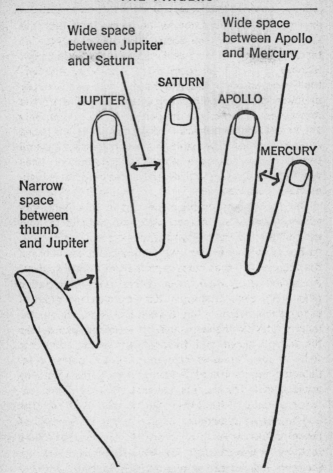

Wide space between Jupiter and Saturn

Wide space between Apollo and Mercury

JUPITER

SATURN

APOLLO

MERCURY

Narrow space between thumb and Jupiter

EXAMPLES OF NARROW AND WIDE SPACING BETWEEN FINGERS

son will not only be liberal but extremely progressive and farsighted in his activities. For example, a public-spirited citizen not only will think about the problems in his local school district, but he will plan solutions, then approach the school board with his recommendations. He will use the **Letters to the Editor** column in his local newspaper as a public forum. He'll find other active ways to express his own views. A broad space between Apollo (the ring finger) and Mercury (the little finger) represents, as this example portrays, freedom and independence of action. A person with this hand structure does what he wishes. He'll vote the Democratic ticket because he is convinced it's the wisest choice, even though all of his family will, as always, support the Republican ticket.

If a wide space exists between Saturn and Apollo, the owner of the hand is very informal and careless in both thought and action. A recent cartoon pictured a young man with long, uncombed hair, untrimmed beard, and uncared-for clothes. He was holding a blank picket sign as he sat on a curbstone under a tree along a city street. His words to an equally unkempt lad lounging beside him were, "Whoever pays for my sign gets my support." Obviously, he had a very wide Saturn-Apollo spread. Completely unconventional, he didn't care at all what path he followed. He evidenced self-satisfaction in the extreme. If there had been just a small opening between these two fingers, the young man would not have been so easy to meet and to persuade, and he would not have been so cheerful about acceding to requests.

On some hands, you will find that all of the fingers

are close together. Their owners are formal, self-centered conformists. If, in addition, the fingers curl inward, you have the hand of an insecure person. "Tight-fisted," they are miserly not only with physical possessions but also with their time and energies. The converse is also true. A person whose hand opens easily, with comparatively even spaces between his fingers, is a spendthrift of his time and energy. He becomes wrapped up in whatever he is doing and loses track of time. He will give of his energy and skill until he has little reserve to fall back on for himself. Financial reserves are difficult to acquire and often his energy is "nervous" rather than real because of his inner drive. (Check for spatulate fingertips—they often accompany this spacing.)

Next, draw an imaginary line across the base of the fingers. Is it fairly straight? Evenly set fingers signify optimism and self-confidence. Does the line dip under the Jupiter finger? This person lacks self-confidence. He's sure that if he comments on the sunshine it will rain. He will belittle his own opinions. If your imaginary line dips under the Mercury finger, you are working with a person who always says the wrong thing at the wrong time. He's the one who tells a fellow employee that his opinions are stupid, then discovers that that same employee has been assigned to supervise his work.

Now check the structure of the fingers themselves. Some will be smooth, and some will have knotted joints (see illustration page 46). Keep in mind the example of movement of currents with which this chapter began. Some people feel that smooth joints are found on young hands, knotted joints on older ones.

This is not true. Those who, as they mature, develop the traits represented by knots, will develop the knots also. Experience will help you to differentiate between naturally knotted joints and those distorted by arthritis or rheumatism.

Close your eyes and run your own fingers up and down those that you are examining. Are there knots on every finger? On just the upper joints? The lower ones? Both? Do the knots appear at the same place on both hands? Your answers again provide insights to your subject's personality. Remember that the representations on the less dominant hand are your subject's innate characteristics, while those on his dominant one show how he is handling them. For

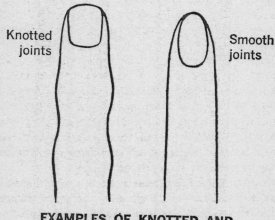

Knotted joints

Smooth joints

EXAMPLES OF KNOTTED AND SMOOTH JOINTS

example, knots on the lower joints of the right, or dominant, hand, when none occur on the left, show that their owner is developing meticulous personal habits.

People with smooth fingers are equipped with antennae which readily bring them ideas and impressions. The field in which they will work most successfully will be indicated by total finger shape and development. Here, intuition plays a role in decision making. These people move quickly, both physically and mentally. When a smooth-fingered businessman happens upon an idea, he immediately senses its ramifications, then relays it to his subordinates for action. He does not take the time to think through its effect on phases of the business other than those with which he is concerned. His own inspiration will drive him to complete whatever parts of the program he must. Most venturesome businessmen are smooth-fingered, but they're supported by knotty-fingered staffs.

Our most skillful public speakers are also smooth-fingered. They can sense the atmosphere and attitude of the group they are addressing and will respond to it. Creative artists in music, painting, and so on, react to feelings and impressions. Smooth fingers again go with this. One fine painter produced beautiful canvases, but had all sorts of problems with the real estate he managed for his living.

Knotted fingers indicate a person who needs to think and reason—these go with "waisted" thumbs. Knots on the first, or upper, joint are "mental" or "philosophic" knots. These show their owner's need to think through problems. Order, consistency, logic in mental activities are present when knots occur on top joints. Legal briefs delight the owners of these fingers. Debate is their middle name. This needn't necessarily be oral; you can be sure these people silently argue their position or their activity in all areas of life. I once went on a trip with a friend who had knots on the top joints. We missed planes and buses because she insisted on arguing with herself and with me about what clothes to wear, which suitcases should be sent ahead, and which suitcases should be carried. Knots on the second, or lower, joint indicate order in material things. Compulsive homemakers are good examples of this. Secretaries with knots on their lower digit joints will keep accurate records, maintain tidy files, and handle correspondence systematically. Their personal appearance will be orderly and clean. Don't waste your time trying to change the minds of people with knots on both joints. Only their own inner forces can do that.

To summarize your examination of the joints, remember that smooth fingers, like water, are fluid, movable, responsive to conditions around them, and that knotted fingers contain barriers to be crossed before events and actions can occur.

Your next observations should be directed toward the length of the fingers on your subject's hands. Measure the Saturn finger from tip to base. This length is approximate to that of the back of the hand from the wrist to the Saturn knuckle on the average-sized hand. Fingers that are noticeably longer or shorter than that denote special traits. Short fingers, like small hands, belong to people who prefer to work with complete activities——they, too, are impatient with details. The phrase "quick thinkers" aptly describes them. They can draw a complete mental picture of a situation or idea from sketchy plans or fragments of thought. Lifeguards at a swimming pool or beach, traffic officers at busy intersections, and sports referees should possess short fingers. Long-fingered people enjoy going into detail and examining situations from many angles. They are the ones who enjoy checking their monthly bank statements very carefully.

Next, note the comparative lengths of the various phalanges. Examine each finger from the front, or palm, side as well as from the back. Check the tips to determine if they are square, spatulate, conic, or pointed (see illustration page 51). Occasionally, you will find they're the same on all of the fingers, but not often. The top phalange, or tip, emphasizes the emotional or spiritual responses of the hand's owner. The middle phalange represents mental capacity and practicality, while the third, or lowest, one is concerned with physical needs and desires. Gourmets, for example, have well-developed lower phalanges, particularly in the back. The more nearly equal the length of these finger segments, the more nearly we find a balanced personality. Experience has shown that each of the fifteen segments (the Mount of Venus is referred to as the third phalange of the thumb) represents its own particular traits.

Recalling again the flow of life currents, you will understand that the more nearly pointed and smooth the finger, the easier for the hand's owner to be aware of and sensitive to the world around him. As Benham expresses it: "——the more pointed the tip the more idealistic the subject, the broader the tip the more practical he will be."[1]

Now let's briefly examine the fingers and their special symbolism. Are most of the fingertips square? Like the square-shaped hand, these are found on practical people. They can become so absorbed with the external world around them that they feel no need for anything else. If the hands happen to show artistic inclinations, the square tips will direct them into functional channels.

Spatulate tips represent activity——the application of mental skills to physical expression. As in the example of spatulate hands previously described, these people are "doers." Cheiro noted, "These people wonder that God took six days to make the world. With the little power they possess, they would revolutionize the world in a day."[2] The patent office is kept busy because of the efforts of spatulate fingertipped people. They're found as headliners in the sports world.

The possessors of conic tips love lofty ideas, elegant clothes, fine food, and beautiful homes. If a woman with conic tips prepares a tray for an ill member of her family, she'll put a flower, a bright napkin, or a gay trinket on it to catch the patient's eye, even though she may burn the toast in the interim. Pointed fingers (in our society you will seldom find more than one or two on a hand) belong to our mystics. Rest-

---

[1] Benham, The Laws of Scientific Hand Reading.
[2] Cheiro, Cheiro's Language of the Hand (New York: Arco Publishing Co., 1946).

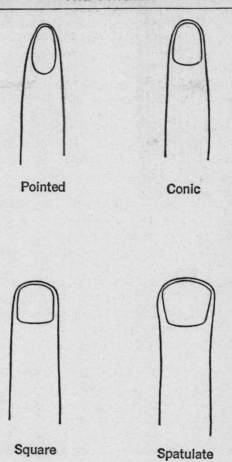

Pointed

Conic

Square

Spatulate

THE VARIOUS FINGER TYPES

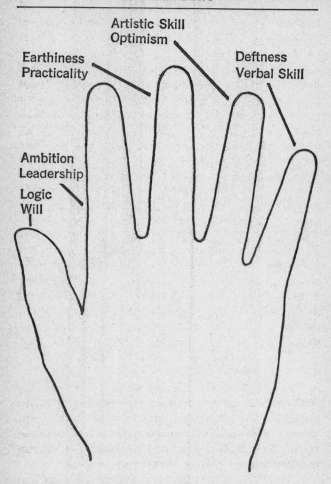

FINGERS AND THE QUALITIES THEY DEPICT

lessness is usually characteristic of these people. Often they seem to be following a Pied Piper the rest of us can't see or hear.

Each finger has its own symbolism, which is a real help in defining personality (see illustration page 52). The index, or Jupiter, finger when well developed reveals determination, ambition, and drive. A normal-sized one will reach to the middle of the first phalange of the middle, or Saturn, finger. Strong executives display Jupiter fingers as long as Apollo ones. Longer than this, the finger belongs to a dictator, a tyrant, or a martinet. If it is crooked, the possessor has little personal honor or integrity. Occasionally, this finger is very short, telling us its owner will search for escape from his humdrum existence. When the first phalange is full and strong, an interest in religion and philosophy is inherent in the personality. When the phalange is short, we note a skeptic. "Ambition, sharp business skills, and the ability to direct others shows in the second phalange."[3] When it is short, there is a lack of personal drive. A strong third phalange emphasizes its owner's sensuality. Food lovers and good cooks, as well as wine connoisseurs, will have strong lower phalanges on both Jupiter fingers—they have the traits indicated, and they've developed them. The milk-toasts of our society have very short third Jupiter phalanges—they have no confidence at all in themselves. Incidentally, mathematical skills show up in this finger. When Jupiter is shorter than Apollo, it belongs to a follower, or partner, rather than a leader.

Turning to the Saturn, or middle, finger, we can

[3] Cheiro, **Cheiro's Language of the Hand.**

describe this digit as the balance wheel. It represents earthy, practical, useful traits. Often it acts as a necessary brake on the other fingers. If it is overly long, the hand belongs to a melancholy person and a misanthrope. Check your own Saturn fingertip. The fact that you have read this book this far means this tip has some flexibility: it's found on those with an interest, though not necessarily a skill, in the occult. The first phalange also represents some intelligent skepticism. If it is very wide, suspect a superstitious side to your subject's nature. The middle phalange represents, when it is long and nicely developed, an interest in agriculture and skills in the exact sciences. The thinner it is, the more pronounced the skills will be in the sciences. Mineralogy and metallurgy are represented in a good third phalange. Possessors of well-developed phalanges here have the ability to concentrate on whatever comes to hand. If it is long and thin, miserliness is present.

Traditional palmistry has taught that equal-length Saturn and Apollo fingers represent a gambling instinct, but this is not necessarily so. However, look for confirming or denying signs in other parts of the hand. If the Saturn finger is definitely shorter than Apollo, its owner will be inclined to all kinds of foolish or thoughtless activities: He might buy the Brooklyn Bridge, an impractical venture, to say the least.

Now for the Apollo, or ring, finger. Apollo, the god of the sun, represents life and creativity. Well-developed Apollo fingers belong to optimistic people. Their top phalange here will be longer than that of Saturn. However, if this finger is longer than Saturn, overoptimism becomes a problem; again, gambling tendencies come into the picture. If this finger is short, shorter than Jupiter, its owner lacks confidence in himself (another way in which various parts of the hand confirm each other). The tip of the Apollo finger is especially important in understanding your subject. When it is square we can look for a love of wealth; long conic tips that incline toward Mercury belong to those who can succeed in some form of commercial art. Artistic intuition reveals itself in well-rounded top phalanges. However, when this phalange is thin and almost bony, look for your subject to be an aesthete. A strong second phalange adds common sense or some degree of practicality to the artistic temperament. Possessors of these are willing to work hard to achieve their goals. Our realistic artists in sculpture and painting, for example, will have firm and even plump development here. The abstract creators, by contrast, will have a long, thin, graceful structure. Common sense is present when a strong middle phalange supports a rounded top one. Competent critics display this element.

A full third phalange tells you that its owner needs to impress other people with his ability. Those who work on Madison Avenue display this trait in their need for public attention. The possessors of strong Apollo fingers also possess charm and personality. Other parts of the hand will tell you whether it is real or whether it is an outward pose, covering insecurity.

Mercury, for which the fourth, or little, finger is named, characterizes speed, deftness, and agility. A long finger is found on those who express themselves well orally. These people need to talk about a subject so that their information and reactions about it come to the fore in a reasonable manner. Often they will not realize how much they know about the area under discussion until they begin to talk about it. As they listen to themselves, they will mentally react, "Oh yes, that is what I think." A large first phalange indicates their verbal skill. On a flexible hand, occasionally, you'll find a short phalange here. In this case, the person is mentally lazy. Editors of all kinds should have long, spatulate Mercury tips.

The middle phalange of the Mercury finger represents business, industry, and the commercial world. When it is long, its owner is practical; when short, he's loyal, if not very wise. A bony Mercury finger should be on a professor in a school of business education rather than an office manager. This gentleman understands theories of economics, but generally cannot successfully apply them. One fine economics professor decided to reform the business world. He went through six jobs in rapid succession before he finally retreated back to his ivied walls.

Most people fortunately display small or underdeveloped third Mercury mounts. For this area of the hand represents negative characteristics of personality, such as cunning, trickery, deceit. When this finger is crooked or twisted, we usually apply the the word sly to it. Such a quality in a criminal poses a problem, but will be an asset to a detective, who also has to be sly. A well-formed Mercury finger accompanies a tactful personality, one who is eloquent in either written or oral expression. A poorly formed one belongs to those who may abuse their knowledge. But, here again, look for other, balancing traits.

As you conclude your observations, check the fingers for flexibility. Stiff fingers represent stiff people. Smooth fingers absorb impressions quickly from the world around them. Long fingers work more slowly and with more concern for detail than short ones. Fingers and mounts together photograph their owners more accurately than any camera.

CHAPTER
FIVE

THE MOUNTS OF THE HAND

Most dictionaries define a mount as a "rise or elevation." Mounts on hands are just that: cushions of flesh at the base of the fingers and around the circumference of the palm itself. They reveal the manner in which the owner of the hand uses his energies and skills, and whether or not he should be employed in other ways. On some hands, mounts are clearly visible; but on others, they are blended, blurred, or concave rather than convex. The Mount of Venus is found at the base of the thumb, marked off from the palm by the life line (see illustration page 60). Lower Mars is directly above it. Continuing around the circle, you can note a mount under each finger; they bear names identical to the digits. On the percussion, or outside, Upper Mars is located underneath Mercury. One contemporary hand analyst feels this should be renamed Virgo because the traits it represents are those associated with that astrological sign. The Lunar or Moon mount lies just below. Across the base of the palm, between it and the wrist, is the Mount of Neptune. Benham devotes 260 pages of his book, **The Laws of Scientific Hand Reading,** to the study of the mounts, so significant does he believe them to be. We'll discuss the mounts briefly and will later indicate how to correlate this data.

On the hands you are examining, note which mounts are prominent, that is, are actually elevations of tissue. Also observe which ones seem to be blended together or are concave. For example, instead of separate mounts under Apollo and Mercury your subject's hand may have one fleshy bulge beneath the space between the two fingers—this is a blended mount. Under Saturn the area may actually be hollow or sunken— this is a concave mount. Make note of any vertical lines on the mounts under the fingers. One such line strengthens the significance of the mount; two indicate strength but not as much as one. Three or more vertical lines weaken the mount while horizontal lines detract from it. Therefore, a grille, or network of crisscrossed lines, on a mount is a detrimental mark. Count de Saint-Gennain believed that unraised mounts could be considered active forces in a hand, either strengthening or weakening various traits, depending upon how they were marked by lines.

As you study the mounts under the fingers, keep in mind the length of the fingers. Long fingers add to the mount. Abnormally short fingers detract from them. Short fingers represent, as we previously discussed,

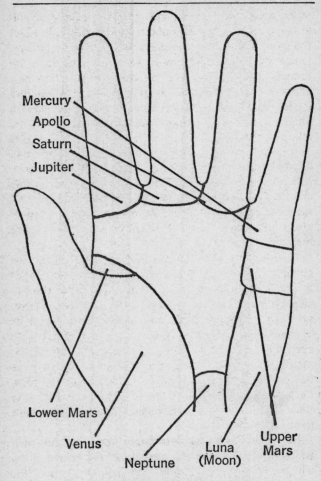

Mercury
Apollo
Saturn
Jupiter

Lower Mars
Venus
Neptune
Luna
(Moon)
Upper
Mars

MOUNTS OF THE HAND

agile thought and movement, sometimes even impulsiveness. If one finger is short, these traits will affect
the mount beneath it. On the other hand, long fingers,
indicating the ability to work with detail, whether intuitively (smooth joints) or consciously (knotted joints),
affect mount influences in another way. A military
leader could well have a hand with short, smooth
fingers and a well-developed Jupiter mount. His quick,
intuitive knowledge of a military maneuver helps him
to lead his men victoriously. Or, a clergyman with long,
knotted fingers and a strong Jupiter mount would be
able to guide his parishioners to acceptance of his
church's creeds because he had thought through their
rationale and development. As mounts lean toward or
blend into each other, their skills and talents are
merged.

Now let's explore the meaning of the mounts, beginning at the top of the hand with Jupiter. As it does
in the finger above it, this mount, named for the ancient ruler of the gods, represents ambition, drive,
pride in accomplishment, and independence, all part
of the Jupiterian personality. Natural leaders, these
people, large in build, although not the tallest of the
mount types, carry themselves proudly, displaying the
self-confidence that is a part of them. Many of them
have a weight problem. This is due in good part to
their love of fine food and wines. The best cooks have
good Jupiter mounts.

The hands of the Jupiter people are firm, full, and
well shaped. If knots are present on the fingers, they
will blend into the total picture and won't mar the
hand's pleasing appearance.

Jupiter women are active outside of their homes. The business world interests them; community activities and charities profit from their leadership.

Religion is important to those with a strong Jupiter development. Their need of an active spiritual life is illustrated by the number of religious professionals with this development prominent. However, they range the whole field, from conservative fundamentalism to active atheism.

No matter what their chosen field, possessors of strong Jupiter mounts will never be content to be part of a crowd. Their individuality demands recognition. Whether it is physical, mental, or spiritual leadership they demonstrate, demonstrate it they will. They have good speaking voices; this is a real help in their leadership roles. They mature early and frequently marry early. Generally, well-defined Jupiter mounts are found on those who prefer mental work to physical, but they display physical drive and energy as well, if necessary, in order to assert their leadership. If the mount is very fleshy or overdeveloped, it indicates vanity and braggadocio. Its owner will be highly conceited. Refer back to your thumb observations in interpreting a Jupiter mount.

A well-developed thumb and Jupiter mount together are a good team, but a small thumb with a strong mount reveals a person who would like to be a leader but cannot carry out his program. On some hands you will note a strong Jupiter finger, but the mount beneath it will be flat and underdeveloped. Actually a better follower than a leader, this person will make a big show of heading a small group to carry out ideas and plans developed by someone else. He's able to pick up and utilize the suggestions of others. In politics, for example, he makes a good committeeman or ward leader, but not a good commissioner. A good Jupiter development combined with a good Saturn development will identify a natural teacher. When the upper phalanges of both fingers are strong, the teacher will become an administrator or will advance to the college level. When the third phalange of the Saturn finger is strong on a Jupiter hand, manufacturing and industry should be the chosen fields.

When you have identified a good Jupiter mount on a creative, or Apollo, hand, you've discovered a talent that can write skillfully about leadership. And combined with Mercury's abilities, a strong Mount of Jupiter reveals vocal leadership. The late Senator Dirksen was the personification of this. His inimitable gravelly tones drew attention, no matter what his subject. Good doctors also combine strong Jupiter and Mercury mounts. The medical mark on the Mercury mount (three to five small vertical lines) strengthens natural skills.

When the Venus mount is as strong as the Jupiter mount, you have identified social workers or those who like to help others to be more attractive. The average operator in a beauty salon will not have this hand structure, but her boss will, if he is successful. A good Moon mount development will increase writing skills and a love of travel, with new faces to meet and places to see.

Because determination, drive, and ambition are indicated by well-built Jupiter mounts, keep in mind the fact that these can create trouble as well as success. Henry VIII of England, the epitome of several kinds of gluttony, undoubtedly had a high, flabby Jupiter mount.

A depression instead of a mount under Jupiter is found on the hand of a person who has no respect for himself or anyone else and is deficient in confidence. He displays a distrust of religion in any form. The more concave the mount, the more negative the traits. But also keep in mind that an overdevelopment of a good trait can be as detrimental as the lack of it. When we've overeaten at a festive occasion, we know that "too much of a good thing" creates its own problems.

Turning to Saturn, we can characterize this mount with the word "independence." Here in America, Abraham Lincoln, with his tall, craggy appearance, his droll, philosophic outlook, and his inner preoccupation, has been cited as a perfect Saturn example. At the other end of the spectrum, some of our best-known criminals are also Saturnians. When you find a hand with this mount displaying prominent development, you will find it belongs to a person who works well alone; indeed, he usually prefers it. Caution is a keyword in his makeup. He questions ideas, information, and decisions. In short, he's a good critic. On this type of hand, it is particularly important to check the finger structure to determine how the Saturn influences can best be managed. If the fingers you are examining are longer than the palm, mental skills will dominate over physical ones. These people may become research historians or chemists, depending upon other influences. When this tip is square, more common sense is present than if it were conic or pointed. The more it flows into a point, the more it reveals its owner's idealism or concern with dreams and superstitions, depending upon the shape of his nail. A spatulate tip tells you that your Saturnian will direct his activities toward the needs of others. If he is in medicine, for instance, he will be looking for new treatment techniques.

A strong Saturn mount combined with a full middle phalange denotes skill in science, math, or agriculture. Farmers who live and work with satisfaction on huge farms have prominent Saturn mounts. Recluses also develop this portion of their hands.

When the lowest phalange is solid, it underscores its owner's ability to concentrate on whatever requires his attention. Often it accompanies a cold, impersonal, often very cruel, nature. The legendary wife slayer, Bluebeard, must have had an enormous Saturn mount and lower Saturn phalange. On most people, the Saturn finger is the longest one and acts as a balance for the rest of the hand. As previously mentioned, all hands need some of the sobering influence of this area. It tempers the exuberance of Apollo and gives a note of weight and seriousness to Jupiter. More hands lack strong Saturn mounts than possess them, thereby depending on the finger itself for balance. When the mount is overdeveloped you will find its owner is a melancholy person, tending to see the dark side of things. The paintings in his home will belong to the realistic school. Many of those with strong Saturn mounts have an interest in music, but generally they interpret rather than create. And they prefer classical compositions or progressive jazz to light popular selections.

Frequently you will find that this mount leans toward or blends into the Jupiter mount. Then, it adds reason or logic to an ambitious Jupiter leader. This is one of the signs to look for on the hand of a would-be diplomat or negotiator. When the Saturn mount leans toward or merges with that of Apollo, it tones down the optimism and lightness of the individual and makes him more realistic. Frequently, cartoonists have Saturn and Apollo mounts similarly developed. When a strong Saturn combines with a full Mercury mount, medicine, particularly psychiatry, is underscored as a profession. Our space program also has many employees of this type; their inventiveness and patience are in demand. Venus people will find that Saturn cools them and helps to control their emotional responses. Saturn salespeople need Venus warmth if they're to be successful in meeting the public. The "Pollyannas" of this world could use a bit of Saturn influence—they would be easier for the rest of us to tolerate.

Strange as it may seem at first glance, many mystics have good Saturn mounts. They are independent of the opinions and influences of others. They work best in privacy. In short, they symbolize what Saturn mounts represent: sobriety and self-guidance.

Skin texture will be particularly helpful to you as you analyze a Saturn mount. Coarse skin combined with a strong mount emphasizes strong and coarse feelings. Riot leaders, bomb tossers, and neighborhood troublemakers display these signs. Smooth or fine skin tempers violent or depressive feelings. A Saturnian will conceal or rise above gloomy feelings and a melancholy outlook if his skin is soft-textured or his hand is flexible. He'll enjoy his Christmas gifts even though he is mentally anticipating a bill for them that will shortly arrive (he'll assume he'll pay for them, as his wife has no funds of her own).

Benham points out in his study that many criminals are found with very strong Saturn or Mercury mounts. These people display an inability to conform to social demands, and they insist on living according to antisocial standards. But don't jump to the conclusion that all of those with strong Saturn mounts have criminal tendencies. It does suggest, though, that these characteristics of Saturn need to be directed into constructive channels.

The Apollo mount, located at the base of the ring finger, like the digit above it, discloses the sunny, versatile, and artistic qualities of personality. It adds color to its owner's existence and underscores his appreciation of beauty in whatever area of life he moves. A love of excitement, gaiety, and occasionally, even frivolity, goes with it. Many old palmistry books indicate that well-developed Apollo mounts point to financial success and wealth, but this is more wishful thinking than actual.

A high, firm Apollo mount tells you its owner loves life and enjoys sharing his pleasure in it with others. His attitudes seem to say, "I'm so glad you included me in." Obviously, this development was in the hand of the poet who reminded us to observe the solid part of the doughnut and not its missing center. (Those with strong Saturn mounts concentrate on the hole.)

When the Apollo mount is overdeveloped, look for other cues in the person's hand. His talents and skills may be overrated. He may try to get by on promises rather than on production. If the mount is concave, you've discovered a dreamer rather than a doer.

We need Apollo mounts to help us relax and to savor the pleasant experiences of life. Fortunately, most of us have enough Apollo development to enable us to enjoy life, but not so much that we can't carry on the world's work.

Contrary to the opinion of many, a well-formed Apollo mount does not mean that its owner is an artist. It does signify, as mentioned before, an awareness of and a need for loveliness, color, and grace around him. There is a story of an old mountain woman who lived in a hut by a pigsty. When asked how she could stand the odor, she replied that if she breathed deeply into the wind she could smell the pine woods further up the hillside. That's an Apollo nature.

Apollo people love excitement of all kinds. They will relish watching a blazing building as much as a play. Holidays were made for them. One man with an overdeveloped Apollo mount quit his job one October so that he would have time to ready his home for Christmas.

Is someone you know a nonstop talker, prattling endlessly on any topic that comes to hand? You can be sure his Apollo mount is a prominent one. It may even blend into the Mercury mount so that you can't readily tell which is which. Often this accompanies a quick temper that scorches everything and everyone around it, then disappears as quickly as it came.

While you're looking for the incessant talker, check also on anyone who considers himself proficient in romance. His attentions will be suave, graceful, and exuberant. Whether man or woman, he will show his feelings with dancing eyes, smiling lips, and sprightly walk, trite as these attitudes may seem. The dashing fictional lovers of literature and films would, if they were real people, have strong Apollo mounts. The next time one of the Gabor women is on television, note her hands—real Apollos!

Almost all Apollo people have eye difficulties. Many wear glasses most of their lives. Contact lenses are a real blessing to them—they can satisfy their natural vanity and still see.

When a strong Apollo combines with a good Lunar, or Moon, mount, this makes known their owner's vivid imagination. Because this supports Apollo's creativity, such a combination is found on the hands of writers, particularly in the fields of adult fiction and children's fairy tales and picture books. Advertising attracts these people, too.

Mercury, the last of the finger mounts, often blends into Apollo, and just as often slips toward the side of the hand. Shrewdness and keenness are synonymous with a high Mercury mount. Hands themselves are important to these people—they "talk" with them. One reason Mercury smokers don't stop using cigarettes or pipes is that they wouldn't know what to do with their hands.

Trial lawyers, typified by the fictional Perry Mason,

also have good Mercury mounts—probably good Jupiter ones, too, if they're going to assert themselves in this way.

One very special marking is located on the Mercury mount. Look for three or four vertical lines on the mount area itself. These are known as medical stigmata and represent skills in the healing arts. However, they do not mean their owner has to be a doctor or a nurse. Dietitians, therapists, counselors, consultants, many teachers and clergymen, are healers of one kind or another. Some workers in occult fields also carry this sign. There are healers without this sign, but their talents are acquired rather than innate. They achieve neither the satisfaction nor the success of those whose hands carry this mark. The man whose hands were discussed in the first chapter, who worked for a meat firm instead of pursuing a surgical career, had the medical stigmata. His inner drives found release when he worked as a first-aid expert. An engineer in a company making photographic supplies and equipment spends his leisure time as a medic for a community volunteer ambulance corps. Naturally, his left hand bears this mark, but it did not appear on the right one (his dominant hand) until he had discovered and developed this outlet for his talents.

Mercurians tend to be shorter than average, but seldom have to watch their weight, even though they may be physically lazy. Most of them are very agile, mentally as well as physically. When sports are part of their life, they will excel in them. And as for playing cards with these people, keep aware of what you're doing. They'll win because of skill and careful observation, even when they don't have "good" cards.

A word of caution is in order concerning hands with an overdeveloped Mercury. When this is in evidence, you will find other clues to reveal an unscrupulous nature. Your subject will deny that this is true of him, so keep the information to yourself. But be careful in future dealings with him. He probably has ten friends whose hands you **must** examine, no matter how full your schedule. He'll maintain he's doing you a favor, giving you a chance to develop your talents!

No matter how modestly they live, those with strong Mercury mounts enjoy making money and putting away a portion of it. They will use their intuition in choosing investments. Business dealings will be influenced by this same intuition. When the Mercury mount extends out over the percussion side of the hand, add unpredictability to your subject's cleverness and adroitness in handling both people and situations.

Many fine dancers have good Mercury mounts. Agility, grace, and an intuitive sense of timing and rhythm contribute to their success.

The underworld is peopled with the owners of large and overlarge Mercury mounts; Saturn runs it a close second. Cleverness, slyness, and trickery are indicated when the mount is oversized and out of balance with the rest of the hand. Coarse skin and a strong Mercury mount on an attorney's hand should warn you to be careful in selecting him to represent you. But if the skin is smooth and fine and the mount is good, have no fear in choosing him.

As with a strong Mercury finger, the mount is found on the hands of eloquent talkers. Salesmen, lawyers, lecturers, and politicians will have pronounced Mercury mounts on one or both hands. The mothers who take the floor at PTA meetings reveal this Mercury drive.

If you have a knowledge of astrology, remind yourself of the general Gemini traits, and you will discover they are the same as or similar to Mercury ones.

There are two Mars mount areas on each hand. Upper Mars is just below Mercury, along the percussion side, while Lower Mars is below Jupiter and above Venus, on the inner side of the palm. Lower Mars falls inside the life line as it begins its trip around the base of the thumb. In the center of the palm is the Plain of Mars. Sometimes you will find Upper Mars referred to as Passive Mars and Lower Mars as Active. The letter "p" in the words upper and passive will help you remember which is which.

Mars, the traditional god of war, suggests aggressiveness and a love of battle and struggle. Underlying these is the ability to stick with a situation and to see it through. This is most important to remember when you relate the meaning of Upper Mars to the rest of the hand. If the percussion side bulges out a definite mount is present. When the mount also shows height, it can be considered strong. If the side of the hand is flat or, in some cases, even indented, then the mount is missing, and the traits it represents are negative or lacking altogether. A good Upper Mars tells you your subject can keep his head under pressure and duress. If the baby is teething and the three-year-old is fretful, the drapes didn't come from the cleaner, the larder is almost bare (payday and shopping day being tomorrow), and your husband calls that he is bringing home a guest, you will cope without going to pieces if your Upper Mars is strong. Pasting modeling clay on it won't help its development—it has to be part of your nature. Those with little aptitude in a particular field will keep trying in spite of obstacles if they have a strong Upper Mars. A lack of development here tells you that the hand you're evaluating belongs to someone who not only gives in when problems arise, but also closes his eyes to possible solutions.

A strong Lower Mars can be identified by a definite bulgy development above the Venus mount and below Jupiter, enclosed by the first part of the life line. If the mount is definitely pink or red, its characteristics are strengthened. Owners of a strong mount here are aggressive "pushers." Unless their heart line is unusually strong they will demonstrate no concern for the rights and interests of other people. Frequently, these people go out of their way to pick a fight. When both Martian mounts are strong, real champions of causes have been identified. Whether their battles are mental or physical depends on the rest of the hand's revelations. However, when Lower Mars is strong and Upper Mars is not, you will have the hands of a bluffer. He'll argue until cornered, then run.

There are other differences between the two mounts. Those with a strong Lower Mars marry early and mature early; they spend their money readily and overindulge in food, drink, and fun. Their approach to life is characterized by traits we tend to classify as "masculine": the "caveman" lover and the rugged, unthinking athlete exemplify this. Upper Mars people, in contrast, marry later and generally mature later. They are more thrifty. More than any other sign they enjoy using their hands in various crafts. They reach their goals through sheer determination and steady persistence. You can argue with most Martians, but don't try to force them to do something against their will. Upsets will occur when you least expect them.

Once again, examine the skin carefully on the hand with strong Mars mounts. If it is smooth and fine, the aggressive qualities and argumentative nature will be revealed in mental activity—an asset to lawyers and clergymen. Wrestlers, stevedores, handlers of heavy machines will have strong, coarse, and sometimes even rough skin. Flexibility reveals more versatility in the person than you might otherwise suspect. You should hope your subject has knotty fingers so that he will think before he launches into a project. When the Upper Mars has fine lines on it, watch out for a temper. All Martians have a temper; some use it wisely, but the small lines weaken the ability to control it. Everyone needs some Mars mount traits. Unfortunately, many people don't always have them in sufficient quantity or in a positive form.

Under the Upper Mars along the rest of the percussion side is the Lunar, or Moon, mount. Like the one above it, this mount should show a definite outward as well as upward fullness in order to be considered well developed. Vertical lines across the mount indicate a love of travel, and, with even a minimal Neptune development, a love of and need of water. These people should live near a stream or pond or shore. Vacations should be spent near or on water.

Even their use of water in drinking and bathing should be a concern if good health is to be maintained.

The amount of imagination and the extent to which it is used is revealed by the Moon mount. Young children will reveal a good Moon mount that flattens down in their dominant hand as they mature. They have disciplined their dreamy nature, or have even subdued their imaginations, usually because of parental influence. Your total hand structure reflects how you will use your Lunar influences. If, for example, your hand is broad and full, the mount will denote the extent of your day dreaming; if your hands are small, your imagination is more likely to be constructive than escapist.

Our great composers and writers have strong Moon mounts—their imaginations or "mental eyes" help them to plan and organize their work.

Question the possessor of a Moon mount very gently about his marriage. He has more problems in this area than other people; at the same time, his home is important to him. These people not only seem cold and impersonal, they really are. Many psychics have strong mounts here. They will be responsive to music and rhythms others are unable to hear. Patience and love are necessary in handling Lunar people. They move in a different world. When Moon traits are tempered by influences of other mounts, then hot tempers, industry, and drive will be cooled down. Action will be slower. But these modifications will enable them to achieve almost impossible goals.

Across the base of some palms, not very many, you will discover a Mount of Neptune. This is a small area that, when present, closes the gap between the Mounts of Venus and Luna. It almost never occurs on knotted hands. The owner of a prominent Neptune mount has more than a normal amount of intuition and sensitivity. He is able to encourage animals and plants to grow; he possesses the symbolic "green thumb." A Neptune mount is found on persons who have ease and grace in physical movement, such as athletes and dancers.

The final mount is Venus, named for the goddess of love and beauty. Marked off from the rest of the palm by the life line, Venus tells you about its owner's need for love and affection. A nicely rounded mount reveals that your subject can give affection or express his feelings for others in a positive manner. He needs also to be loved and cared for. Generosity is synonymous with a strong Venus mount. Both sensuous and sensual, it humanizes cool personalities. An overdeveloped one tells you that you're working with someone to whom promiscuity can be a problem, even though he may not consider it so. Venus people must be with other people, both for business and for relaxation. They will impulsively and openly display their pleasure with their surroundings and their associates.

A low, tight Venus, by contrast, goes with a calm, collected, self-contained nature. When someone with this hand development marries, it is seldom for love but for security, either financial or emotional, or mutual interests. Be sure to check the mount structure in both hands. Sometimes you will find a full-rounded Venus on the less dominant hand and a flattened one on the dominant one. (This is a good illustration of the fact that use doesn't develop hands; inner experience does.) This means that if middle-aged or older, the subject has warm feelings for other people but has closed them off, usually because he has been deeply hurt. He has built a wall around his inner feelings and acts out a role depicting the person he wants the world to think he is. On a young person's hand, this difference in development sugests that he has not yet had enough time or experience to receive or give the emotions he needs to express. On some older hands, you will find grilled lines or loose skin, suggesting that the mount was once full, and a generally worn appearance. This is the sign of a profligate, who has wasted or abused his emotional appetites.

Venusians enjoy all kinds of beauty, particularly music. This doesn't mean that they can create or interpret it, but they need it as an element in their lives. They rest more comfortably with soft background music. When possible, they acquire record libraries for their own pleasure. The best professional musicians have good Venus and Lunar mounts.

A pink color always accompanies a good Venus mount. When it becomes yellow, physical problems are always present.

Finally, again remember to look at the mount as part of a whole hand and combine the characteristics you see. Flabby, inert hands with full Venus mounts tell you their owner's adventures are primarily in his head. Firm hands with knots on the upper joints bespeak their owner's disciplined handling of people and things he loves. Stiff hands and full mounts belong to sensual people who will indulge their appetites at whim. A marriage in a justice's office sans flowers or friends is fine with them; they just want to get it over with.

If you remember that the Mount of Venus could be considered as the third phalange of the thumb, you will recall that this area of the hand shows will, reason, and affection or love. A strong firm Venus mount reflects all of these.

CHAPTER
SIX

THE THREE MAJOR LINES
OF THE HAND

"My life line isn't very long. Does that mean I'm going to have a short life?"

"Will I get married? How many times?"

"What does it mean if my head line and heart line meet?"

"Haven't I got a marriage line?"

These and a myriad of other questions will come your way as soon as your friends discover that you can "read their palms." Such questions reflect the general impression most people have of hand analysis: that the lines are what give information, and that's all there is to it. Valuable as they are, the lines are not the most important components of hand analysis. But they do make a special contribution, and that is what we are about to examine. Not all people are affected in the same way by similar events, so their hands will not react in the same way. As you read the lines of the hand, you will learn about its owner's abilities, talents, skills, and patterns of activity.

Keep in mind the advice given in the first chapter: information revealed to you in one part of the hand can be confirmed in another. The lines in the hands are not developed by physical use but reflect changes in the life of their possessor. "Lines in a hand are the direct reflex of the subject's mind, and . . . his mind produces, controls or alters them."[1] When a person's life takes a new and different direction, or he deliberately decides to change a trait or characteristic, this will be reflected in his hand. The lines do change, sometimes they will disappear and, often, change their direction. New ones may develop. By taking palm prints periodically and comparing them, you can note even small changes as they occur. In both hands of a middle-aged woman, the life and head lines were separated at their beginning by a full quarter-inch. She was appointed to a new position which made it necessary for her to think and plan at least six months ahead, if her work was to be successful. This forced her to alter some of the routine in her private life as well as in her work. Within a year the space between the head and life lines on her right (dominant) hand closed. As she changed her life-style, the lines changed accordingly.

Not only does the length of a line have meaning; so does its width and depth. Note also the color of the lines, whether healthy pink, deep red, blue, or even white. Observe whether the line are clear or broken.

---

[1] Benham, The Laws of Scientific Hand Reading.

Some will have islands: the line splits into two branches and comes together again. These always represent a period of problems or difficulties. Branches running down from the lines draw strength away from them. A square on a line, particularly at a break, is a good sign. On a break, it's like a bandage: a healing or mending influence. Always be sure to compare the line in both hands. Many fine lines sprayed across the palm are signs of sensitivity. These hands look as though they had been rubbed with steel wool. The lines in the less dominant hand are the road map of their owner's life, showing the directions he will be most likely to follow. The lines in the dominant hand show how the life trip is progressing and what changes are occurring. Remember again what was stated in the first chapter: the hands reveal; they do not force. You are not a dreamer because your head line says so, it says so because you are.

The life line begins between the thumb and the Jupiter finger, cuts out into the palm, circles the Mount of Venus and goes down toward the wrist or around the thumb. Sketch the one you are examining on a blank outline of the palm or mark the line on the palm itself with a soft pencil so that you know how far it cuts into the palm and the direction it takes as it nears its end. Note any breaks, branches, or islands (see illustrations pages 82 and 83).

A short life line indicates that its owner should live by his wits rather than his fists, figuratively speaking. When the line is short in both hands, check the wrist bracelets; these also give an indication of life spans. A good fate line also represents additional years. When

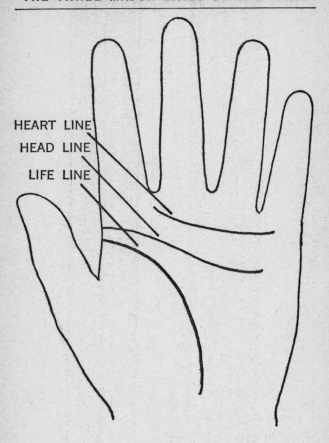

HEART LINE
HEAD LINE
LIFE LINE

**NAMES AND LOCATION OF THE
THREE MAJOR LINES**

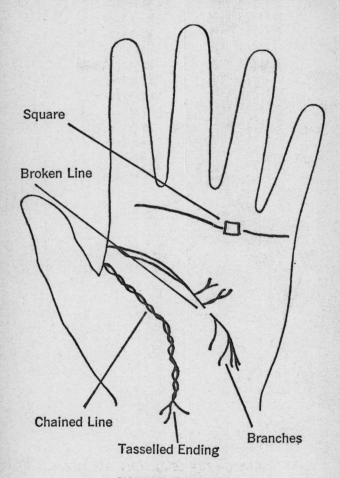

Square

Broken Line

Chained Line

Tasselled Ending

Branches

VARIOUS SIGNS

the line is clear and doesn't have many breaks or islands, it tells you the owner likes and needs lots of action—his vitality is amazing. Sometimes the owner of such a hand will say, "But I have lots of physical problems! My health isn't that great!" He's still around, isn't he? A person with less natural strength and vigor would have succumbed long before.

The closer the life line stays to Venus, the more mental the person's activity. This person prefers parlor games to outdoor ones. When the line is "chained" or made up of many islands, poor health is indicated. Sometimes you will find a life line that is badly broken or crossed or islanded at the beginning, then clears as it goes along. Each problem will be overcome, and the latter years will be better. Be sure, as always, to compare both hands to determine the possibilities here. When the less dominant hand has a shorter life line than the dominant one you can be sure this means that the length of the physical life has been increased and that vitality and interest in life have also increased. With medical advances and increased knowledge of nutrition has come the lengthening of life lines generally in our Western culture.

Does the bottom portion of the line circle around the base of Venus? Even though its owner may enjoy travel, he needs roots; a home base is essential to him. When the line flows toward Neptune or Luna it belongs to a restless wanderer. He not only wants to travel, he needs to. Horizontal lines on Venus strengthen this yearning.

Check on the depth of the life line. The deeper it is, the more easily its owner can throw off worries and concerns. He can keep his head in an emergency. When the line is thin, its owner will be a nervous person. His endurance, both physical and mental, is low. Sometimes a person that you think is lazy really isn't. Take a look at his life line: a thin one will tell you he just can't keep going. A broad but shallow line means the same thing.

Next, check the beginning of the life line. In some hands, this one and the head line start together and continue in that way for as much as an inch, or out as far as the Saturn finger. Then the life line turns on its downward path while the head line ventures out into the palm. On other hands, there is a gap between the beginning of the two lines. On some hands, you will find one pattern on the dominant hand and another on the less dominant. When the lines are joined, you know that your subject, when a small child, was dependent upon and close to his parents or whoever was responsible for raising him. He relied on them to make his decisions. The longer the lines are joined, the longer this dependency lasted. Parents of these people were usually reluctant to allow them to mature. "Mama knows best" is the influence they grew up with. As adults they need to think before they act.

If a woman with this kind of hand mark buys a dress on the spur of the moment, she'll be unhappy with it even though the price is low and the dress is suitable for her. She'll question and debate and generally worry about it. She may as well return it, because she won't be happy with it.

A driver with this kind of hand will cautiously approach an intersection with a green light and will brake and come to a stop even before the amber light appears. By contrast, the driver whose head line and life line begin with a wide gap between them will unerringly sense when it is safe to go through, and he won't jam on his brakes and create a pile-up of cars behind him. For when a space exists between these two lines, you're dealing with a person who at a very early age thought for himself. His decisions will be made instantly. He sees a suit, tries it on, buys it——no belaboring or long cogitation. However, in a situation when he feels he has to think, he shouldn't. For him, the expression "He who hesitates is lost" holds true.

On a particular pair of hands, you may find a separated type of construction in one hand and a merged construction in the other. Remember the example at the beginning of this chapter. This person has changed his approach to life, either consciously or unconsciously. Don't attempt, even if your subject asks you, to say which course is right. That is his decision. But whatever construction occurs, his less dominant hand shows how he should make decisions that are crucial.

Lines that cut across the life line mean problems. A series of five lines denotes countless worries. A real break indicates an accident or major illness. When this occurs only on the less dominant hand, the problem has been handled well or the causes of it have been removed. Whenever an island occurs, strength and vitality are lessened during a difficult period, but return in full force when it is over.

On some hands, you find lines paralleling the life line on the Mount of Venus, inside the life line. These are influence lines and indicate that someone very close to the subject has a great effect on him. When the influence line appears at the beginning of the life line, for example, it probably represents a parental figure; when it occurs further down it represents a teacher or trainer who has been unusually important, or a spouse, etc. Occasionally, several influence lines appear in the same hand. This person needs support from those around him to bolster his own confidence. Islands in the middle segment of a woman's life line suggest menopausal problems. These are disappearing in our culture, again because of medical advances. As the line descends toward the wrist, sometimes branches occur (see illustration page 83); these diminish strength and vitality. As the line nears its end, sometimes it forks or tassels, showing that the life forces will fade gradually. If the ending is abrupt, the life will end that way.

And how can you tell when events will take place? There are several ways to tell time by hand analysis, but they are complicated and require much study. Try this for a simple device. It will not give you an exact time, but it is a good approximation. (If you want a more accurate technique, any detailed hand analysis text will give it to you.) Measure the front of the middle phalange of the Mercury, or little, finger on the less dominant hand. You can use a part of your dominant hand as the measuring stick. Now mark off along the life line segments equal to this length. Each one will represent **about** twenty-three years. Thus, a line measuring three complete segments plus a little more would show a total of approximately seventy-five years. This is an estimate, but for most purposes it serves.

We had mentioned that you should observe color in lines. A pink life line represents a healthy body and circulation. Red lines suggest strong feelings, desires, and tempers. When the lines are yellowish, digestive problems should be a concern. Blueness is caused by poor circulation and a lack of oxygen in the system. Thin, cold, blue lines you're not likely to see—such people haven't enough interest in life to care much about anything, let alone having their hands read. Very rarely you'll find a hand that has no life line. Their owners live on nervous energy and have little real vitality. Equally rarely you'll find a life line that begins high on Jupiter. Its owner is ambitious far beyond the norm and has problems disciplining his energies.

Now let's move on to the head line (see illustration page 82). The length, depth, and direction of this line will indicate to you not only the amount of thinking power or mentality your subject has, but also will indicate how he has used it, which is really more important. A comparison of both hands again shows changes. When the line is short in the less dominant hand and longer in the other, the subject has developed his mental capacity. If the opposite is true, he has not used what he had and, therefore, has lost some of his ability.

We've already discussed cases where the head line begins at or near the life line, under the Jupiter finger along the inside edge of the palm. In such a case, the sooner the head line pulls away from the life line, the earlier the owner began to think for himself. The longer they are tied, the older the person was before he developed (or was allowed to develop) self-confidence and self-reliance. When the head line follows the curve of the life line and bends way down into the palm, suspect mental instability. If the two lines closely parallel each other, serious problems exist.

Generally the head line leaves the life line at about twelve years of age and goes across the palm toward the percussion side of the hand. The kind of line that most people would consider a good one would slope slightly as it neared the Lunar mount. If it began above the life line, it would signify a great sensitivity in the subject. Persons with this construction are confident in their own ability and are deeply hurt when others show a lack of faith in them. When these lines are separated at their beginning, be sure to check the fingers for knots. Smooth fingers increase the intuitive sense, knotted ones restrain it a bit. If the head line begins far up on the Jupiter mount, unusual or outstanding leadership is evidenced. Occasionally you will find a head line that commences inside the life line, on the Mars mount. This person has a terrible time making up his mind, if indeed he ever does. Some politicians apparently have this: they can't take a stand on anything.

Note whether the line slopes gently across the palm, goes straight, or bends upward. If it slopes downward, many of your subject's characteristics, traits, and abilities have been inherited from the family of his parent of the opposite sex. If you're working with a woman's hand and her head line slopes down, she has received her makeup from her paternal ancestors. Conversely, if it slopes up, she has received her makeup from her maternal progenitors. When the line is fairly straight, the legacy of personality comes from both sides almost equally. This information is often of help when you work with children, in determining what guidance and direction to give them. A straight head line denotes a love of details. The longer it is the fussier its owner. For some reason, if any artistic skill is indicated in another part of the hand, a straight head line generally signifies a certain amount of success in commercial endeavors.

Now make note of the length of the head line. The further it reaches across the palm the more versatile its owner's mind. A long one will extend at least beyond the Apollo finger. It is short when it ends under Saturn; this belongs to a person with a one-track mind. One young man became enamored over telephones when he was quite small. He developed a communication system with several buddies, using waxed cord and tin cans. He went on to develop all sorts of wired and wireless hookups, and finally he landed in trouble when he tried to tamper with the regular telephone system. His eyes still gleam when someone asks him about phones—an authentic one-track mind. I have every confidence that he'll end up working for the telephone company in some capacity. His head line ends just below the middle of Saturn.

When the head line goes into Upper Mars, you're dealing with a person filled with common sense. The more it bends to the Moon mount the more imagination comes into the picture. Again, here is a specific sign helpful to speakers, writers, and artists of all types. Both strong mental skills and imagination, vital in these fields, are present in good supply. Most strong psychics have good Moon mounts partially bisected by the head line. Once in a very great while you may discover a head line that reaches to the Moon mount, only to droop there very badly, then end in a chain of small islands or a star (see illustration page 105). This indicates real mental difficulties, even to the point of mental disturbance. A nursery school teacher who was a student of hand study had problems with a new student. She discerned a mark of this type in his hand and asked for his previous school records. These showed that an illness had left brain damage, difficult to diagnose, according to the specialists who treated him, but apparent in his palm.

Now determine whether or not the head line is deep, clear, shallow, chained, or broken. A deep, solid, clear line indicates a good memory and self-control. Often an even temper, because of mental discipline, goes with it. If the line is deep and long, but broken, the mental stamina or staying power is also broken. When the line is chained, or made up of many islands, it belongs to a worrier. If only the dominant hand looks this way, you would be wise to caution your subject to slow down and let someone else assist with his decisions. He has been under an extraordinary amount of pressure.

On some hands, the head line will be quite thin and narrow. It tells that its owner doesn't like to use his mind very intensely; he can be easily argued out of a position. He may be bright, but he can't seem to use his abilities. Again, compare the hands to see if changes have occurred—it's very possible. Broad lines suggest this type of mental ability also. Incidentally, if the head line is changed, don't be surprised if the subject assures you that he has lots of headaches.

You'll observe a head line with breaks or gaps in it on some hands. This means its owner has lapses or gaps in his judgment. Old palmistry books claimed this meant an early death. But actually, if such a fate did occur, it was because the unlucky fellow didn't use his head.

Branches rise and descend from some head lines. Those that flow toward the heart line are good and indicate that the subject is trying to improve in ways represented by the mounts toward which the lines are directed. Branches descending draw away mental strength and spirit. The area where the split begins shows what is influencing your subject. If it occurs under Apollo, for example, it reveals his concern in the arts and his desire for recognition here. As with the life line, breaks are a real problem. You can never depend on such a person. When the break is surrounded by a square, this is a temporary situation that will pass. Squares are, in a sense, like bandages in hand analysis (see illustration page 83).

Some hands that you examine will have a merged head line and heart line. We'll go into that as we describe the heart line itself. On a very few hands you may discover a double head line. These people lead two or more lives; they're versatile and amazingly astute in handling people. Successful career women who manage an office and a family competently often display a double head line. An entertainer who can headline in Las Vegas and at the same time hold the reins on a business venture has the same marking.

Above the head line is the third major line: the heart line (see illustration page 82). Between the two on the majority of hands is an area called the quadrangle. When wide, it represents a broad, open mind; and, when narrow, just the opposite. These people make up their minds and never change them. Followers of Franklin D. Roosevelt may have been liberal in their views during the years of his Presidency, but those who still cling to those same views, thinking that they are still applicable, have narrow quadrangles. Time has swirled around them, but they haven't changed.

The heart line begins on the percussion side of the hand under the Mercury mount, travels across the hand above the head line and below the mounts, and ends in the area of the Jupiter mount. It indicates the depth of a person's emotional nature and the manner in which his emotions react to various situations. A word of caution: Do not confuse it with the passionate feelings expressed by the Venus mount.

Most heart lines are below the mounts a distance equal to the top phalange of Apollo. When it is closer to the mounts than that, its owner is not known for subtle, deep, or intense feelings. Most of them are pretty obvious people. Heart lines usually curve a bit as they move across the hand, bending distinctly upward as they near Jupiter. This upward swing belongs to people who need to express their feelings through action. For example, when one of her neighbors died, a woman with this upward curve prepared dinner every night for the grieving family and their guests. However, she never made a formal call. Her actions expressed her sympathy. There's one major exception to this: If the Mercury mount and finger are strong, a husband will make a fancy speech as he delivers a necklace to his wife on her birthday. Other men would forget or look a bit sheepish as they made the presentation. Strong Mercury development and an upward swing to the heart line denote a need to express feelings verbally.

When the heart line is on the short side, ending underneath Saturn, it reveals cool affections in the owner, who seems to be impersonal in his relationships with both co-workers and family. A short line is occasionally combined with a full Venus development; this indicates a great deal of sensuality. There is an abundance of physical sexual drive but little accompanying delicate emotion.

By way of contrast, on other hands the heart line may end between Saturn and Jupiter. This points out those who instinctively sense emotional reactions in others, both positive and negative. These people get along well with their associates. A businessman will sense that his secretary has a personal problem and will overlook her long lunch hour. A wife will prepare her husband's favorite dinner, sensing his need of special attention.

On some hands, the heart line goes all the way across to the opposing side of Jupiter. It reveals that its owner knows both great joy and great sorrow. He feels deeply and is unable to control his feelings. For example, he may inform everyone around him of the status of his love life.

Many heart lines curve upward and fade away between Jupiter and Saturn. This indicates such a person's contentment with his emotional life. These individuals accept other people and situations for what they are. One businessman had two employees who were incapable of performing their duties as well as the others on his staff; they simply didn't have the same kind of abilities. For political reasons he had to retain them. He did not get upset when they failed to perform well. He knew they could not plan ahead, and he understood that they did not handle other people easily or well. They were quick to complain or find fault, but this was part of their nature; they were not even aware of it. He accepted them for what they were and did not waste time and energy belittling or berating them. He praised them for what they did accomplish.

Some heart lines are clear and smooth, indicating simplicity in emotional approach. Others are chained or filled with islands—here emotional troubles exist. When the line is thin and difficult to detect, it belongs to someone who is disloyal to anything and everything. He'll follow whatever course seems most expedient. Branches descending from the line represent disappointments; ascending ones, particular satisfactions. Some experts say upward branches indicate an optimist and downward ones a pessimist.

When checking the heart line, more than any other line, it is important to examine both hands. On a right-handed person the right hand shows immediate response or reaction to the emotions, while the left indicates the subconscious reaction. Most women display this clearly. And, again, check the color of the line. A pale line clearly states: pale emotions. A red one reveals a quick temper and a lack of emotional discipline or control.

Occasionally, you'll find hands where the head line and heart line are blended into one. In medical terms it is called the simian line. Whenever you find it, you have found a person with a special problem. Part of the time he will react to people and situations only with his mind, impersonally and intellectually making decisions and thinking his way through situations, without concern for the feelings of the people involved. Then, just when his family and associates have become used to this approach, he will change and begin to respond and react emotionally. When you try to work with him you don't know whether you're going to get an ice-cold, impersonal response or a warm invitation to sit down and discuss your situation. He often doesn't know which way he's going to respond, either.

Husbands who have wives with this kind of hand deserve sympathy from the rest of us. This, along with what are called "feminine" reactions to internal stimuli, creates some really rough situations. For example, one week when her husband calls that he's been detained, Sandra is sympathetic and keeps his dinner warm. The following week she will slam down the receiver and ignore his needs. Incidentally, many people with this sign are very bright and talented—look for indications of this.

Once in a while you will find a heart line with a

branch connecting it to the head line. This indicates that the emotional life is controlled by the head. A student with this marking will see nothing out of the ordinary when his parents sacrifice themselves so that he can proceed with his education. If you ask your subject to close his hands slightly, you can tell at a glance which is stronger, the head or the heart line. Again, check both hands for possible changes.

These three lines—life, head, and heart—are surrounded by others. Lesser lines can modify or strengthen them. (These will be discussed in the following chapter.) Lines can change as the concepts they represent change. This factor helps to make their study most interesting and valuable.

CHAPTER
SEVEN

SECONDARY LINES

In addition to the three main lines of the hand, the head, the heart, and the life lines, there are several others that may appear on the palm. Some hands will exhibit portions of several of these secondary lines, others may have some of them well marked, while a third group will have few marks other than the basic three. There is no guide or rule that states what you will usually find. Every pair of hands will be different.

We'll begin the examination of these secondary markings with the fate, or ambition or Saturn, line (see illustration page 99)—it goes by all of these names. Rising at the base of the palm on or near the Neptune mount, and crossing the palm on a slight slant toward the Saturn mount and finger, it is read from the wrist upward. It indicates if and how its owner may achieve worldly or material success. When

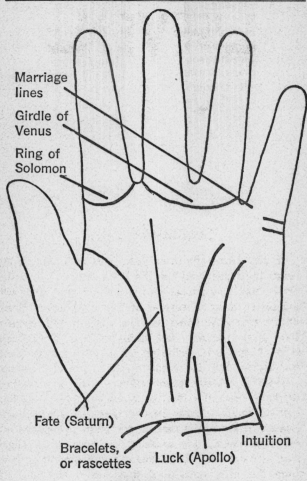

Marriage
lines

Girdle of
Venus

Ring of
Solomon

Fate (Saturn)

Bracelets,
or rascettes

Luck (Apollo)

Intuition

SECONDARY LINES

99

the line is completely missing, the possessor of the hand has practically no chance of ever accomplishing anything; he will procrastinate about everything. If the line touches or merges with the life line, it indicates a necessity for that person to have a definite goal or purpose in his life. Mere existence is intolerable. He must live for something specific. If the line stops at the head line, the person lacks the mental ability or agility to attain the success his other talents may suggest. Some say bad luck dogs this fellow. When the fate line terminates at the heart line, lack of emotional control may be the deterring factor. If the fate line begins near the heart line and runs a short distance, success will come in old age. Sometimes this line goes to the Jupiter mount. In such a case, the person's ambition will be altered, changing the course of the career involved. When the line cuts clearly into the mount, outstanding success is quite possible. A thin fate line in the Jupiter area combined with a good head line is found on the hands of those who will not see their own name in lights or listed in **Who's Who** but who have the skill and native knowledge to help others to find success. Ideally, counselors should have this kind of marking.

Sometimes called the line of Apollo and sometimes the luck or Sun line, this rises on the Moon mount, parallels the fate line and ends on the Apollo mount. It is almost never found on the hands of mentally retarded people. A strong line reinforces the head line and signifies mental dexterity and alertness. If it is chained, meager success in life is the best to be hoped for. When broad, the success is superficial and shallow. Possessors of good Apollo lines should be cautioned against taking for granted their natural talents. They need to use industry and determination to win the success that can be theirs.

At the top of some hands can be found one of the most interesting of all lines, the Girdle of Venus. When complete, it resemble an arc running under Saturn and Apollo. Even partial ones can be an asset. Their owner responds emotionally to all kinds of stimuli. The following example illustrates what it represents. Some people can try to manipulate a puppet, but it remains fabric, cord, and wood. Others can play with it and make it come to life—it moves and talks and dances. We respond with pleasure to the personality it projects. The latter persons have a Girdle of Venus. The famous ventriloquist Edgar Bergen projects personality in this way into his puppet friends. People with a strong Girdle of Venus give names to inanimate objects: their car is "Joe" or "Mary," never "it." Such individuals tend to see other people as they want them to be. In short, they project their own personality into them. Whether or not this is good depends upon many other factors. Writers and artists produce more sensitive work when this girdle is present. A double or triple girdle denotes extreme sensitivity.

Across the wrist are the bracelets, or rascettes. These signify two things: length of physical life and the condition of the reproductive system. Count the bracelets. Each line represents about thirty years of life, so two strong ones and a partial third indicate about seventy years. This is a way to check on a life line. A short line accompanied by several bracelets means that a life of average length can be anticipated.

Strong lines indicate strength in the reproductive organs. When, in a woman's hand, the first one (nearest Neptune) is islanded, broken, or grilled, difficulties in conceiving and childbearing can be expected. If the line is badly broken, serious problems exist.

Breaks in the second line in a woman's hand indicate menopausal problems. Again, as always, check both wrists. Modern medicine can correct problems so that you might observe them in one hand and not the other. Hysterectomies are usually revealed by a break, or island, on the second line. In a man, virility is indicated here. The Mount of Venus and the bracelets show whether you're dealing with a libertine, a Lothario, or a frustrated bon vivant! Or maybe he's really a spirited creature who combines his search for love with physical discipline.

Under the little finger along the percussion edge are the marriage lines, or lines of affection. They represent strong emotional attachments. Because legal matrimony is a man-made institution, these lines may or may not result from such an attachment. Although these lines are not reliable in showing how many such alliances will take place, they do indicate the deep impressions on personality that such attachments can create. Some people are capable of only one such deep alliance; others are geared for several.

Vertical lines crossing the marriage lines have traditionally represented children. However, modern contraceptive devices and fertility drugs have in many cases modified or negated the course that these line markings indicate.

Once in a while, you will find a vertical line on the Lunar, or Moon, mount. This is the line of intuition and signifies stronger than average psychic skills. These people need a religious or spiritual philosophy in their lives. They may or may not find it in an organized religion. They need a creed that allows them to grow, expand, and develop spiritually, not because of impending tragedy but because of basic personal needs.

There is a wide variety of small signs which we will review briefly:

A line of Mars appears inside the life line and serves to strengthen it.

Medical stigmata were discussed along with the Mercury mount.

A Ring of Solomon bends around the base of the Jupiter finger and signifies unusual wisdom, understanding, and intuition.

Stars are bright, exciting signs. Their location too is important, for they reinforce the mount or line on which they appear. On Jupiter, for example, they signify extraordinary ambition. (See illustration page 105.)

Crosses occur when two small, random lines intersect. Tradition gives them all kinds of meanings: a happy marriage if they appear on Jupiter, for instance. But serious study doesn't bear out such views. Generally, they signify mysticism if well marked, or superstition if poorly traced.

Grilles, as indicated in an earlier chapter, are never

beneficial. They make difficult traits worse and detract from positive ones. If one appears on Saturn's mount, it indicates periods of deep despondency or depression. "They grilled me!" indicates that the speaker underwent a difficult questioning period. Frequently, a grille is found on Venus, where it reveals a special need for love and affection.

Triangles have always been considered positive signs. Seldom are they found on people who do not have better than average minds. Diplomacy and tact are associated with them. Many Phi Beta Kappa members have triangles on their Saturn mounts. On the Moon mount, they reveal outstanding intuition and sensitivity.

Once in a great while you may uncover, or rather discover, a trident—an unusual but very positive sign. It signifies a person who lands on his feet regardless of the problems he must work through. However, his success will be in his work, not in his emotional and love life, which frequently is in a sorry state.

Tassels on the end of any line are weakening forces (see illustration page 84). Senile people develop them on either the life line, head line, or both. It was indicated in an earlier chapter that squares, wherever they appear, are good—they heal, strengthen, and generally improve the area in which they're found.

Turn the hand you're examining upside down and look at the fingertips. If tiny droplets of flesh hang down, these emphasize sensitivity.

If you keep in mind that vertical lines (except for the head and heart lines) improve or strengthen, and horizontal ones detract, many of the lesser signs are

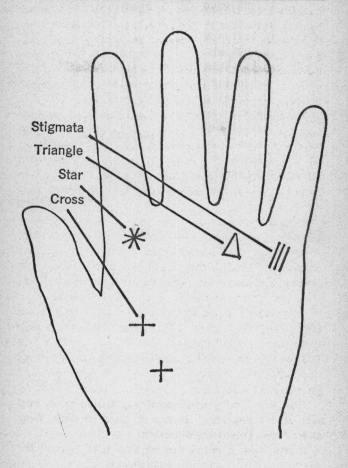

Stigmata
Triangle
Star
Cross

ADDITIONAL SMALL SIGNS

105

easier to remember. "Star-crossed" lovers can be identified by their hands.

Islands in a river interfere with a free flow of water. In a hand, they do the same thing: they interfere with the force of the area in which they occur. After they are passed, full strength recurs.

All these lesser signs need to be considered in the final analysis and the weight of their evidence considered.

CHAPTER
EIGHT

HOW TO UTILIZE YOUR KNOWLEDGE

How do you actually read or interpret what you see in a hand as you sit facing the person who has asked you for this information? It's not as difficult as many would have you believe. (There is a Hand Analysis Checklist in the Appendix that will help you to know what to look for.)

Begin by actually taking in your own hands those you are examining. Carefully look at them individually, front and back. Note their size, skin texture, color, and shape. Compare them to each other, and look for obvious differences. Stroke the backs of the hands, and feel the fingers in pairs, on both hands simultaneously. Some people find they can do this more accurately if they close their eyes and "see" with their own fingers.

Then trace the lines with your own dominant index finger or mark them with a soft pencil. Put a circle around the most prominent mounts. Check on the number of bracelets. Look for any triangles, squares, stars, crosses, or grilles that are present.

Now begin to talk with your subject, explaining to him why his hands provide information to you, and tell him what you are studying. Don't try to remember everything all at once. Admit you are a student and that you are only ready to look for certain things. For a few weeks, try only to study sizes, shapes, and textures. As you develop confidence and your skill begins to be evidenced, add a few more elements: shapes of hands and fingers, nails, knots, a few characteristics of the thumbs. Go slowly and ask, when possible, if your subject will confirm your diagnosis. Ideally, written notes will help. Prepare them after you've completed your work. If you have a palm print, write your notes on the back of that.

As you continue to work and practice, you'll discover that you gradually are acquiring the ability to subconsciously "see" information. This is when extrasensory perception enters into your reading. As you touch the hands and concentrate on them, you will find that impressions and feelings and information come to you. Is it transmitted telepathically? Do you "sense" rather than "read" it? How much can you tell from physiological signs, and how much do you acquire through some other means? Does it really matter? The whole purpose of hand analysis is to acquire insights into the personality that may help improve, channel, or develop it.

In the same way, when a teacher gives a test, only part of its purpose is to determine what factual information has been acquired. Another important reason is to discover what overall concepts have been developed and whether or not a student has adopted good study attitudes. Much more is made known to the teacher than the mere attainment of factual answers.

Many people who study hand analysis use it as a means of developing their own extrasensory perception, a valid undertaking. It isn't necessary, of course, to use hand analysis as a path into a larger field; it's an area of study all its own. However, for those who wish to use it in this way, it's a great door. As you feel others' hands and permit yourself to relax, you will discover that all kinds of impressions may come to you. You may sense events, traits, habits. You will have to sort them, examine them, and share them with your subject. Ask for verification.

Generally, one of the first psychic impressions you receive from a hand concerns color. You feel that certain colors strike a responsive chord. Perhaps your subject should have yellow in the rooms where he is active and involved. (Saturn people generally need yellow for the bright uplift it can give them.) If the subject asks you where you see such information, admit you don't know, but that you feel it. The need to be around water, to be able to relax near water, to love to travel over water is another impression you frequently can sense. Look for confirming qualities— a firm but slightly hollow palm, fingers that curl up a bit and that stay fairly close together, and dry skin. Also, the Apollo finger will generally be conic. What impressions you receive are not as important as the fact that you can use your psychic skills to go beyond a physiological study.

Sometimes you will look at hands and feel that you see absolutely nothing. This happens to all of us on occasion. Just offer your regrets, and invite your subject to try again another time. Actually, there are some hands that seem to say almost nothing. But then, their owners are not particularly complex or interesting people. And there are those who seem to be convinced that you aren't telling them everything, that you are able to see all sorts of dire things and just don't want to tell. Often these are the people who have very little in either their hands or in their lives. Brush aside their questions and urgings and tell them that you are still a student and haven't yet developed the skill to interpret hands as difficult or complex as theirs. They'll be delighted with the compliment—and with you.

We have not described the techniques of making palm prints. To do it simply, ink the palm with a large stamp pad. Rub the corner of the pad into the center of the palm so that you obtain a complete impression. Place a piece of plain white paper on a pillow. Carefully put the inked palm on the paper. Then, with your opposite hand, push the pillow up into the palm so that you print the entire picture. Generally, you need to re-ink the thumb and take a separate impression of it—it usually doesn't print evenly with the rest of the hand because of its location. A little cleanser removes the ink from the skin.

On the back of the print, write the date and a brief description of the elements of the hand you can't reproduce: size, texture, shape, and so on. You'll discover that details will show up in the print that you missed in the visual examination. File away your prints so that you have them to compare with future prints of the same hands. Then you can note the development of changes.

All through this study we've used terms and names that are shared with astrology. The two studies have much in common. Both offer ways to discover more about a human personality. The names in both studies have the same or similar connotations. Some experiments have been made using both fields. Not long ago a party for twelve people was held to which an astrologer and a hand analyst were also invited. Each guest had supplied the hostess with vital statistics of his birth. Brief horoscopes were prepared in advance. As the hand analyst interpreted hands, the commentary was tape-recorded. Then the two readings were compared. For nine guests, the analyses were in complete agreement and except for words like "houses," "squares," "trines," "lines," "mounts," and "knots," they sounded practically alike. One of the three remaining guests was given two widely divergent readings. But he admitted he didn't know the hour of his birth and had just picked one at random, and that because he had been born in a mountainous area of North Carolina and his mother had died, there was even a question as to the exact date of his birth. When he was soon thereafter able to supply correct information, the two readings came into about 75 percent agreement. The readings for the two remaining guests were 70 to 80 percent in agreement. On the whole, it was a highly successful performance. Don't hesitate to use astrology and hand analysis together.

A final word: As you work with hands, you'll discover that you can use the information they give you in casual and informal ways. Look at the hands of committee members at the next club meeting you attend. Mrs. X keeps her hands in front of her mouth —she'd really like to hide behind them. Miss Y is quietly twisting a hanky into knots—she's a nervous, tense person. Mr. Z is busy clenching and unclenching his fists—how insecure he must be!

Make it a point to shake hands with those you meet. Even that brief touch will give you information. Reading hands can be fun and exciting as well as helpful. Happy reading!

APPENDIX

HAND ANALYSIS CHECKLIST

Check the items that describe the hand you are examining. Check the list for both hands. Then go back and read the interpretation for what you have checked. This will help you to remember what the various parts mean. With a little practice, it will become habit.

ENTIRE HAND

General Appearance
Large
Small
Average
Broad
Narrow
Dominant Hand Larger
Less Dominant Hand Larger

Scarred

Texture
Smooth
Rough
Thick
Thin
Dry
Moist

Color
Pale
Pink
Red
Blue

Flexibility
Stiff
Firm
Pliable
Flaccid

Type
Elementary
Square
Spatulate
Conic
Pointed
Mixed

THUMBS

Long
Short
High
Low
Wide Set
Close Set

Square Tip
Spatulate Tip
Conic Tip
Pointed Tip

Straight
Waisted
Rigid
Flexible

FINGERS

Generally Smooth
Generally Knotted

Space between Thumb and Jupiter
Space between Jupiter and Saturn
Space between Saturn and Apollo
Space between Apollo and Mercury

Jupiter Very Long	Jupiter Very Short
Saturn Very Long	Saturn Very Short
Apollo Very Long	Apollo Very Short
Mercury Very Long	Mercury Very Short

Jupiter

Smooth
Knotted

First Phalange Longest
Second Phalange Longest
Third Phalange Longest

Square Tip
Spatulate Tip
Conic Tip
Pointed Tip

Apollo

Smooth
Knotted

First Phalange Longest
Second Phalange Longest
Third Phalange Longest

Square Tip
Spatulate Tip
Conic Tip
Pointed Tip

Saturn

Smooth
Knotted

First Phalange Longest
Second Phalange Longest
Third Phalange Longest

Square Tip
Spatulate Tip
Conic Tip
Pointed Tip

Mercury

Smooth
Knotted

First Phalange Longest
Second Phalange Longest
Third Phalange Longest

Square Tip
Spatulate Tip
Conic Tip
Pointed Tip

MOUNTS

Jupiter

Full
Concave

Leans to Saturn

Star
Cross
Triangle

Saturn

Full
Concave

Leans to Jupiter
Leans to Apollo

Star
Cross
Triangle

Apollo

Full
Concave

Leans to Saturn
Leans to Mercury

Blends with Mercury

Star
Cross
Triangle

Mercury

Full
Concave

Leans to Apollo
Blends with Apollo

Star
Cross
Triangle
Medical Stigmata

Upper Mars

Full
Bulges to the side

Star
Cross
Triangle

Lower Mars

Full

Star
Cross
Triangle

Venus

Full
Flat

Smooth
Lined

Firm
Flabby

MAJOR LINES

Life

Begins with the Head Line	Smooth Pink
Reaches to Neptune or Wrist	Chained Red
Reaches halfway down the Palm	Broken Yellow
Square on the Line	Deep Blue
Star on the Line	Shallow
Cross on the Line	
Ends in a Tassel	

Head

Begins on Jupiter Mount	Deep
Begins with Life Line	Shallow
Begins above Life Line	
Descends into Palm	Merged with Heart Line
Cuts straight across Palm	
Rises toward Heart Line	Double Head Line
Reaches beyond Apollo	Square on the Line
Reaches to Saturn	Star on the Line
	Cross on the Line
Smooth	Branches Ascend
Chained	Branches Descend
Broken	

Quadrangle

Narrow	Red
Wide	Pink
	Pale

Heart

High—near the top of the Palm	Smooth
Low—deep in the Palm	Chained
	Broken

Ends on Jupiter	
Ends between Jupiter and Saturn	Red
Ends beyond Jupiter	Pink
Ends between Saturn and Apollo	Pale

Merged with Head Line
Branched to Head Line

LESSER LINES

Fate, Ambition, or Saturn Line   **Apollo or Sun Line**

Ends at Head Line   Strong
Ends at Heart Line   Chained
Begins near Heart Line

Girdle of Venus   **Bracelets**

Whole   Complete
Broken   Broken
Double or Triple Girdle

Marriage or Affection Lines   **Ring of Solomon**
Line of Mars

BIBLIOGRAPHY

Benham, William G. **The Laws of Scientific Hand Reading.** New York: Duell, Sloan and Pearce, 1946.

Bright, J. S. **The Dictionary of Palmistry.** New York: Bell Publishing Company, 1958.

Cheiro. **Cheiro's Language of the Hand.** New York: Areo Publishing Company, Inc., 1964.

Compton, Vera. **Palmistry for Everyman: An Outline of Chirology.** Westport, Conn.: Associated Booksellers, 1956.

Gettings, Fred. **The Book of the Hand: An Illustrated History of Palmistry.** London: Paul Hamlyn, 1965.

————. **Palmistry Made Easy.** Hollywood, Calif.: Wilshire Book Company, 1966.

Hutchinson, Beryl B. **Your Life in Your Hands.** New York: Paperback Library, 1967.

Niles, Edith. **Palmistry; Your Fate in Your Hands.** New York: HC Publishers, Inc., 1969.

Peckman, Elizabeth. **Your Future in Your Hands.** New York: Ace Publishing Corporation, 1968.

Squire, Elizabeth Daniel. **The New Fortune in Your Hand.** New York: Fleet Press Corporation, 1960.

$1.00

The
**Character
Analysis
Handbook**

A valuable guidebook to understanding people through
handwriting, palmistry, astrology, body language, fashion,
and a number of what are often considered "general
characteristics."

Valerie Moolman

What Does
Your Handshake
Reveal
About You?

THE CHARACTER ANALYSIS HANDBOOK

Would you believe that a handshake, the shape of a nose,
the color of a person's eyes, and the length of the big toe
are all revealing factors in determining the character of
an individual? These and a wealth of other interesting
checkpoints are covered in this thorough compendium
based on extensive research by psychologists, psychiatrists,
and industrial fact-finders. No curious person should be
without this handy guide.

▼AT YOUR BOOKSTORE OR MAIL THE COUPON BELOW ▼

THE PSYCHIC SCIENCES
THREE IMPORTANT BOOKS DEALING WITH THE SPIRITUAL AND THE MYSTICAL
by BETH BROWN

The Truth About Mental Telepathy

In this era of wonderment concerning vibrations, messages sent via the air waves, and other unknown powers that put individuals and thoughts together, these well-written documents come as reassurance of the fact that mental telepathy is a part of our daily life. Beth Brown helps the reader to accept this power and to understand it.

Your Words Are Your Magic Power

What you say and how you say it are vital factors in the way you live your life and in the results you achieve through friendships, business, romance, marriage, and every other facet of your existence. The author cites case histories of failures being transformed into successes through the turn of a phrase, and offers the reader a feeling of inner strength through faith in himself.

The Power Behind Your Dreams

Dreams are more than happenstance, and there is unanimous accord among the great psychologists of the world that your dreams are a key to your past and a clue to your destiny. Beth Brown has spelled it out simply with the hope that more people will make themselves aware of the power behind their dreams.